IMAGINATION AND THE LIFE OF THE SPIRIT

SCHOLARS PRESS
POLEBRIDGE BOOKS

edited by
Robert W. Funk

Number 2
IMAGINATION AND THE LIFE OF THE SPIRIT
An Introduction to the Study
of Religion and Literature
Lynn Ross-Bryant

IMAGINATION AND THE LIFE OF THE SPIRIT
An Introduction to the Study of Religion and Literature

Lynn Ross-Bryant

SCHOLARS PRESS

Distributed by
Scholars Press
101 Salem Street
Chico, CA 95926

IMAGINATION AND THE LIFE OF THE SPIRIT
An Introduction to the Study of Religion and Literature
Lynn Ross-Bryant

Library of Congress Cataloging in Publication Data

Ross-Bryant, Lynn.
    Imagination and the life of the spirit.

    (Polebridge Books: no. 2)
    Includes bibliographical references.
    1. Religion and literature. I. Title.
PN49.R73   1980   809'.9352   79-28464
ISBN 0-89130-377-4
ISBN 0-89130-378-2 pbk.

Printed in the United States of America
            1   2   3   4   5
        Edwards Brothers, Inc.
    Ann Arbor, Michigan 48106

FOR ELLIOTT

CONTENTS

ILLUSTRATIONS

Figure		Page

ACKNOWLEDGMENTS

Such a book on religion and literature must begin with an acknowledgment of the crucial importance of the ever-growing body of scholars whose work gives shape to this field and to the creativity of the theologians, philosophers, and literary artists who are called upon in this study. Only with this background and this creativity was it possible for *Imagination and the Life of the Spirit* to be written at all.

In addition, I would like gratefully to acknowledge the importance of numerous students, colleagues, and friends who encouraged and supported me in the development of this book. The faculties and students of the California State University, Chico and the University of Southern California shared their ideas with me in this project; Patricia Chapla of Chico and Rui Sadamura of Los Angeles typed the various drafts of the manuscript, the editors and staff of Scholars Press aided me with their enthusiasm and editorial assistance. I am especially grateful to a special group of friends—Giles Gunn, Stanley Hopper, David Miller, Charles Winquist, Anna Winquist, and my husband Elliott Ross-Bryant—who read the manuscript, or portions of it, shared their wisdom and their criticism, and nourished the growth of my ideas by their conversations and friendship.

Grateful acknowledgment is made of the kindness of the publishers and authors who have granted permission to quote from the following material:

Waiting for Godot by Samuel Beckett, Copyright 1954 by Grove Press.
I and Thou by Martin Buber, translated by Ronald Gregor Smith, copyright © 1958 by Charles Scribner's Sons.
God's Presence in History by Emil L. Fackenheim, copyright © 1970 by New York University.
Naming the Whirlwind by Langdon Gilkey, copyright © 1969 by Langdon Gilkey. Published by Bobbs-Merrill Company.
Christ and Apollo by William F. Lynch, S.J., copyright © 1960, University of Notre Dame Press, Notre Dame, Indiana 46556.
After the Fall by Arthur Miller. Copyright © 1964 by Arthur Miller. Reprinted by permission Viking Penguin, Inc.
The following poems by Theodore Roethke: "The Light Breather," copyright © 1950 by Theodore Roethke; "The Manifestation," copyright © 1959 and "In a Dark Time," copyright © 1960 by Beatrice Roethke, administratrix of the Estate of Theodore Roethke; "Moss-Gathering," copyright © 1946 by Editorial Publication, Inc. from *The Collected Poems of Theodore Roethke*. Reprinted by permission of Doubleday & Company, Inc.

Part One
RELIGIOUS AND LITERARY
EXPRESSIONS OF A CULTURE

Chapter One
INTRODUCTION: THE STUDY OF RELIGION AND LITERATURE

Works of the imagination of a particular culture reveal much about the life of the spirit of that culture. They tell the story of who the men and women of that culture are: what they value, what they fear, what they dream of. Literature of a particular time and place also reveals much of our story through the way we respond to the stories of other people. Literature opens for us the truth of what is and the possibility of what might be, and the response we make to it is formative of the truth and possibility of our own lives.

This study of the relationship between religion and literature presupposes that literature is an important revealer of religious dimensions of a culture and that by taking account of the religious dimension of experience our understanding of a work of literature will be deepened. This understanding assumes that religion and literature are two different things, and to confuse them would do an injustice to both. On the one hand, this means that literature will not be read as a theological exposition with characters and plot added to it. Nor will literature be judged by the standards of truth or logical organization appropriate to theology. On the other hand, literature will not be seen as a substitute for religion. The general approach will be to assume that aesthetic experience is not religious experience. Through close attention to particular works of literature and to theological insights we will hope to understand more about religious dimensions of a culture. In the novel *The Horse's Mouth* Joyce Cary records this conversation about art:

I'll show you how to look at a picture, Cokey. Don't look at it. Feel it with your eye. . . . And first you feel the shapes in the flat—the patterns, like a carpet. . . . And then you feel it in the round. . . . Not as if it were a picture of anyone. But a colored and raised map. You feel all the rounds, the smooths, the sharp edges, the flats and the hollows, the lights and shades, the cools and warms. The colors and textures. There's hundreds of little differences all fitting in together. . . . And then you feel the bath, the chair, the towel, the carpet, the bed, the jug, the window, the fields and the woman as themselves. But not as any old jug and woman. But the jug of jugs and the woman of women. You feel jugs are like that and you never knew it before. Jugs and chairs can be very expressive. . . . It means a jug can be a door if you open it. And a work of imagination opens it for you. . . . I'm trying to teach you a big happiness.[1]

This discussion is about a painting, but the same ideas can be applied to a study of literature. Through close, careful attention to the shapes and contours, the form and structure of a work of the imagination, a door is opened. A door is opened to the uniqueness of particular things and people and events and to a universal quality of these particulars that reveals something of the way things are and how they might be.

We discover not only something about another culture through the study of literature but also something about ourselves. Who we are, and the culture out of which we come, will make a difference in how we read literature. Just as the time and place out of which a work comes provide its grounding, so our own time and place establish ours. We bring something to every poem we read, every painting we look at. We are not simply passive receivers before a work of art. We must enter into the creative process if the door is to be opened.

This involvement in the process, coupled with the power of symbols to open various levels of meaning, raises an important point we must keep in mind as we approach literature. People say of a work of art—a painting, a poem—"Well, that's what *I* got out of it; that's what it means to *me.*" The intent of such a statement is that there is no more to be said; *my* response is all there is for me. It is completely subjective and therefore impossible to talk about with another person. "If you get something different out of it, that's o.k. It's what it means to you that's important." There *is* some truth in statements like these. We all are different; we all do

[1]Joyce Cary, *The Horse's Mouth* (New York: Harper & Brothers, 1944), pp. 98–99.

bring our own particularities to a work of art. Language and thought operate in such a way that we *cannot* escape completely our own subjectivity. We cannot apprehend the object before us—the work of art in this case, though we could say the same thing about all objects of human knowledge—as it is *in itself*. We must interpret. And in interpreting, we bring our own point of view, our own assumptions. Our own presuppositions present the world to us in a particular way, and we know things only through our own eyes.

However, to emphasize only the subjective aspect of interpretation is to forget that there is something *there* to interpret. Something is given that is carefully structured and that guides interpretation. We must attend to what is given if we want the work of imagination to open a new world to us. A novel, if it is a good work of art, has a definite structure with consistent development of characters and plot that reveals *something*—not *anything*. Its symbols are multivalent—having a cluster of meanings—but not just *any* meanings we choose to apply to them. There is always a remainder with a work of art or a symbol within a work of art that cannot be analyzed away. This is the nature of symbols. But symbols grow out of a certain context and lead to a particular point. They open a unique door that we, through attending carefully to what is given in the text, may discover. And through this we will learn something about the particular culture out of which it is written and something about ourselves as human beings.

The works of art on which this study will concentrate will be literary, with occasional references to other art forms. This is simply to make the study more manageable; all works of art can be equally powerful in revealing religious dimensions of culture. The literary and theological works we will examine come primarily from modern culture. Thus, as we explore understandings of religion and literature and their possible relationships, we will also be moving toward an understanding of our own culture and its religious dimensions. Our study will be, then, about the relationships between religion and literature and how those relationships are revealed in our culture. Since religion and literature both rely on symbolic expression, one of the recurring themes will be the power and importance of symbolic language for understanding religion and literature in modern culture.

In chapter two we will examine the nature of religious experience and its expressions in traditional cultures and in the modern period. We will be especially interested in how we, as modern women and men living in "secular" culture, understand religious experience. We will also explore contemporary formulations of the relationships between religion and culture. In chapter three we will look at this question from the point of view of literature and examine ways literature has been related to its culture and religion, concentrating on the modern period in Western culture. We will see what artists have revealed about culture since the seventeenth century and how developing values of Neoclassical, Romantic, Victorian, and twentieth century literature reflect and transform their cultures. It is during this period in Western culture that Christianity lost its power as the focal point of society and science took on a dominant role in culture. We will explore the effect these developments have had on literature and religion.

It is because of these developments that a study of the relationships between religion and culture, in our case particularly literature, is important in our time. With this background, in part two we will devote our attention primarily to artistic works and theological thought of the twentieth century. In this way we will focus even more particularly on the manifestations of religion in our culture. Using this material we will examine four possible ways of discussing the religious dimensions of literature. These four angles of vision are not intended to be exhaustive, nor can one be used to the exclusion of the others. Nonetheless, they will provide tools for examining the literature of our time and will also give insights into the religious situation of the contemporary world.

The four approaches are as follows: (1) Religious Themes in Literature. This will involve a study of traditional religious symbols and myths as they are embodied within a work of art. We will examine how different critics develop this method, what their presuppositions and intentions are, and what several specific themes and symbols reveal about the modern world. (2) Literature as Possibility. Looking at literature as a hypothetical creation, both structurally and thematically, we will see what possibilities art presents to us. The importance of possibility to both religion and literature will be explored. (3) Literature as Dialogue. Speech and communication—or, very often in modern literature, the lack of them—are important in revealing the possibilities of affirmation within a novel. Dialogue is also important in literature as story-telling and as the ability to organize one's life meaningfully by being able to relate it in story form. This is associated with the sacred stories of religion. Dialogue, as a key to relationship, is also seen by several theologians such as Martin Buber and Gabriel Marcel to be at the heart of the religious experience. (4) Literature as Mythopoesis. This view stresses the mythic side of literature, asserting that by the transformation of myth through poetry, the power of myth is once more made available for us.

Imagination and the Life of the Spirit is, then, both a study of various relationships between religion and literature and a tool for exploring religious dimensions of contemporary culture. Of course, the intention of the book is not to define all possible relationships between religion and literature or the religious climate of our time but to stimulate the imagination to make its own journey. The forms of imagination and the life of the spirit are not static entities that can be defined once and for all. Rather, they are growing, transforming processes that constantly invite and require our growth and transformation.

Chapter Two
HUMAN EXPERIENCE
AND THE SACRED

Through the history of human beings there have been many different expressions of the nature of the sacred, the relationship of men and women to the sacred, and the connection between experiences of the sacred and the secular in human life. These expressions have taken the form of myths, or sacred stories, which traditionally have provided a structure of meaning and value for human existence. In this chapter we will examine some of these expressions as well as the loss of meaning and value that has appeared frequently in the modern world as the power of myths has diminished for many people. With the loss of the power of sacred stories to unite the people of a community with each other and with the sacred, a disjunction between religion and culture—one's religious life and secular life—has often resulted. It has been the task of many contemporary theologians to attempt a reformulation of a vital connection between religion and culture. This chapter, then, will provide a background for our understanding of religion and will set the stage for raising the question of the relationship between religion and the literature of a culture.

DEFINITION OF RELIGION

It is difficult to provide one definition of religion that will encompass all the various experiences that have been designated as "religious." There is a danger that in reducing religion to one basic, universal definition, one is more apt to lose the uniqueness and power of the actual experience than to enrich one's understanding of religion. Nonetheless, we must explore common elements that have been considered to be a part of this experience if we are to discuss religious dimensions of literary works.

We will focus on four characteristics that are dominant in most descriptions of religious experience. First, religious experience involves an immediate awareness of something that transcends the realm of ordinary experience and ordinary ways of comprehending experience. This does not necessarily mean that the experience does not involve the events and things of ordinary experience, but rather that a new dimension is added to our perception of them. This may be called the experience of the sacred, the Wholly Other, the Ground of Being, the Ultimate, God. Second, the result of this encounter is a transformation of the person who experiences it. This transformation generally involves the total person; all of one's being is affected. Third, because of the totality of the involvement, this is an extremely intense experience. And fourth, out of this intense transformation, one's understanding of the whole of things, one's world view, is changed. Along with this, one's way of acting in the world is altered. Thus, there is a transformation of the way one sees the world and the way one acts in it because of an experience of something that transcends one's ordinary experience of the world.

It will be useful to examine how some historians, sociologists of religion, and theologians have discussed these four elements of religious experience. Joachim Wach describes religious experience as:

> a response to what is experienced as ultimate reality. . . . [It] is a total response of the total being to what is apprehended as ultimate reality. . . . [It] is the most intense experience of which man is capable. . . . Religious experience is practical, that is to say it involves an imperative, a commitment which impels man to act.[1]

The element of ultimacy in its relation to human understanding is described by Gerardus van der Leeuw:

> The religious significance of things, therefore, is that on which no wider nor deeper meaning whatever can follow. It is the meaning of the whole: it is the last word. But this meaning is never understood, this last word is never spoken; always they remain superior, the ultimate meaning being a secret which reveals itself repeatedly, only nevertheless to remain eternally concealed. It implies an advance to the farthest boundary, where only one sole fact is understood:—that all comprehension is "beyond"; and thus the ultimate meaning is at the same moment the limit of meaning.[2]

---

[1]Joachim Wach, *Types of Religious Experience Christian and Non-Christian* (London: Routledge and Kegan Paul, 1952), pp. 32–33.

[2]G. van der Leeuw, *Religion in Essence and Manifestation,* trans. J. E. Turner, 2 vols. (New York: Harper & Row, 1963), 2:680.

Van der Leeuw goes on to say that "*a strange, 'Wholly Other' Power obtrudes into life.* Man's attitude to it is first of all *astonishment,* and ultimately *faith.*"[3] In using the terms "Wholly Other" and "astonishment," van der Leeuw reminds us of Rudolph Otto, who uses these terms as well as the word "numinous" to describe the experience of the sacred, of that which is holy and wholly other. Otto uses the Latin phrase *mysterium tremendum et fascinosum* to try to reveal the experience of the sacred, which he claims, can never be adequately described conceptually but can be known only by experience. *Mysterium* refers to that which cannot be known, the mystery before which we stand in fear and wonder. *Tremendum* indicates what inspires this fear, which is not to be equated with being afraid but with being filled with awe. The "Awe-fullness" of the holy inspires in us "creature-feeling," which is "the feeling of personal nothingness and submergence before the awe-inspiring object directly experienced." [4] But it is not only awe or dread that we experience in the presence of the holy. *Fascinosum* indicates the wonder that is also part of the experience. The religious experience for Otto is the entrance into the presence of the holy.

Frederick Streng also talks about the element of ultimacy in defining the religious, and he adds as well the elements of transformation and the new way of seeing the world and acting in it that follow from the experience.

> Religion is a *means of ultimate transformation.* In this definition, the focus is on the *religious* character of human awareness, which includes at least two elements: ultimacy and effective power. . . . The religious concern is practical: it not only *asks* but answers, or purports to expose, the most profound meaning of existence. The problem of existence is how to be *real.* To "be real" means to *know* what is true and right, to translate knowledge of truth into aims, and then to have a *means to perfect* these aims.[5]

William James also discusses religious experience in terms of what is real:

> It is as if there were in the human consciousness a *sense of reality, a feeling of objective presence, a perception* of what we may call "something there,"

---

[3]Ibid., p. 681.

[4]Rudolf Otto, *The Idea of the Holy,* trans. John W. Harvey, 2nd ed. (New York: Oxford University Press, 1958), p. 17.

[5]Frederick J. Streng, *Understanding Religious Man* (Belmont, Calif.: Dickenson Publishing Company, 1969), pp. 4, 2.

> more deep and more general than any of the special and particular "senses" by which the current psychology supposes existent realities to be originally revealed.[6]

The intensity of the experience is referred to here, and it is also certainly evident in Otto's *mysterium tremendum.*

The quality of religious experience that describes the involvement of the total person is affirmed by Paul Tillich. He speaks of faith as "ultimate concern."

> [It] is an act of the total personality. . . . Faith is the most centered act of the human mind. It is not a movement of a special section or a special function of man's total being. They all are united in the act of faith. But faith is not the sum total of their impacts. It transcends every special impact as well as the totality of them and it has itself a decisive impact on each of them. . . . Faith as the embracing and centered act of the personality is "ecstatic.". . . "Ecstacy" means "standing outside of one-self"—without ceasing to be oneself—with all the elements which are united in the personal center.[7]

Thus it is not reason or emotion or will alone that is involved in the religious experience but the total being of the person. Religion is not one compartment of life but embraces and grounds the whole of life.

MYTH AND RELIGION

One way to understand how this experience of the sacred is given form within an individual's life and the life of the community is through a discussion of myth. "Myth" is a term that often is equated with "fairy tale" or "fable," signifying something not "true." As the term is used in the study of religion, however, it indicates a sacred story, an account of why things are the way they are, where life comes from, what is meaningful in its passage, and where it is going. A myth is a story of the gods, of that which transcends or grounds human existence and gives meaning to it. Myth explains, in terms of the ultimate, how it is that life is meaningful and whole, how all aspects of existence are related to each other because of their relation to the sacred. That which meaningfully relates existence is authoritative. It is that to which we look for how we should understand and live our lives. And it is *true*; it is what is really real. The ritual recital, and often reenactment, of this story is a way of entering into the presence of the

[6]William James, *The Varieties of Religious Experience: A Study in Human Nature* (New York: Random House, 1902), p. 58.

[7]Paul Tillich, *Dynamics of Faith* (New York: Harper & Row, 1958), pp. 4, 6–7.

gods, into the realm of the sacred. In doing this the participants enter into the power of the gods and into the sphere of meaning.

Mircea Eliade discusses several of the elements we have mentioned in his description of myth:

> Myth narrates a sacred history; it relates an event that took place in primordial Time, the fabled time of the "beginnings.". . . Myth tells only of that which *really* happened, which manifested itself completely. . . . Myths describe the various and sometimes dramatic breakthroughs of the sacred (or the "supernatural") into the World. It is this sudden breakthrough of the sacred that really *establishes* the World and makes it what it is today. [8]

Myths provide the connecting link between the originating, sacred events and the everyday, secular world people must live in. All the various elements of human life and the life of nature are meaningfully intertwined with each other and with the sacred, as long as the exemplary models described in the myth are followed. We see an example of this in the *Enuma Elish,* the Babylonian creation myth, which accounts for the creation of the natural and social worlds and connects them with the sacred.

> When a sky above had not [yet even] been mentioned
> [And] the name of firm ground below had not [yet even] been
> thought of;
> [When] only primeval Apsu, their begetter,
> And Mummu and Tiamat—she who gave birth to them all—
> Were mingling their waters in one;
> When no bog had formed [and] no island could be found;
> When no god whosoever had appeared,
> Had been named by name, had been determined as to [his] lot,
> Then were gods formed within them.[9]

Tiamat is the salt sea, Apsu the fresh water, and Mummu cloud banks and mist. From the primeval waters are born the gods and goddesses. They represent the different aspects of the world (e.g., the sky and earth, winds, storm, and air). All of creation comes from the primordial waters, which are also referred to (in a nonanthropomorphic form) in Genesis 1:1-2, "In the beginning God created the heavens and the earth. The earth was without form and void, and darkness was upon the face of the deep; and

---

[8]Mircea Eliade, *Myth and Reality,* trans. Willard R. Trask (New York: Harper & Row, 1968), pp. 5–6.

[9]"Enuma Elish," trans. Thorkild Jacobsen in Henri Frankfort, et al., *Before Philosophy,* cited by Cornelius Loew, *Myth, Sacred History, and Philosophy: The Pre-Christian Religious Heritage of the West* (New York: Harcourt, Brace & World, 1967), p. 19.

the spirit of God was moving over the face of the waters." From the first union came other unions until all that is was created. Thus, there is a basic unity between all the things of creation.

There is also a unity between the social organization of people in the world and the divine realm. This is revealed in *Enuma Elish* as a later god, Marduk, wrests control from Tiamat and becomes the chief ruler:

> Thou art the most honored of the great gods,
> Thy decree is unrivaled, thy command is Anu.
> Thou, Marduk, art the most honored of the great gods,
> Thy decree is unrivaled, thy word is Anu.
> From this day unchangeable shall be thy pronouncement.
> To rise or bring low—these shall be [in] thy hand.
> Thy utterance shall be true, thy command shall be unimpeachable.
>
> .   .   .   .
>
> We have granted thee kingship over the universe entire.
> When in Assembly thou sittest, thy word shall be supreme.
> Thy weapons shall not fail; they shall smash thy foes!
> O Lord, spare the life of him who trusts thee,
> But pour out the life of the god who seized evil.[10]

In human terms this becomes the model for kingship. As there is the creation of a socio-political realm among the gods so should there be among human beings. This provides the justification and sanctification for the human social order *and* its connection to the cosmic order. Through myth there is a unity between the sacred stories of a people and their secular lives.

MYTH AND THE MODERN WORLD

In the modern world this unity between our sacred and secular lives has often been lost. Myths are commonly identified as stories that are not true and, lacking truth, they are no longer authoritative models for our lives. Whereas in earlier societies myths were considered true because they explained the way things really are, our society tends to assert that what is true is what can be proved by certain established methods. What is true is what is testable; it is what is predictable. We can, of course, define truth in exactly this way; and then we will have to find another word to describe what is meaningful in life that cannot be proved scientifically. We cannot get to the most important things about caring for another person through scientific means. We cannot assert that

---

[10]"Enuma Elish," trans. E. A. Speiser in *Ancient Near Eastern Texts*, ed. James Pritchard, cited by Loew, p. 23.

life or human life or our lives have any ultimate meaning from an empirical perspective. This is not to say that empiricism is not important or useful in our understanding of life. But it cannot satisfy completely or finally our search for what it means to live. There are "limiting questions" that science cannot ask because the means of answering them are simply not part of its function.[11] The religious questions that are answered in myth are some of these. Whether we choose to call these answers "truth" is not very important. What *is* important is that we recognize that these answers deal with the most significant questions of meaning and value, as these are understood in terms of the ultimate.

Questions about meaning and truth are not unique to modern human beings, but our particular discussion of them in terms of empiricism and myth is. We have an understanding of the world that archaic people simply did not have. They knew nothing of relativity theory or scientific techniques. Nor did they have our understanding of "myth." It was not until the nineteenth century that anthropologists, archeologists, and historians of religion opened the world of archaic peoples by uncovering the past life of human beings and through the discovery of tribes who had not been exposed to the modern world and so lived much as their ancient ancestors had. With these discoveries and the study of the stories these people told that explained who they were and why they were, came the understanding of myth not as a fable but as a sacred story.

But what are the consequences of this understanding for modern human beings? To an archaic person, when the stories of the gods were recited there was no sense of relating a "myth." People were simply telling their true, sacred story. It was a story that dealt with "religion," but religion was connected with the rest of life. The stories of the sacred revealed how one was to live in the secular world, which was a world created by the gods. The situation of modern human beings is often quite the opposite. One's religious life and secular life are often two distinct areas that have little to do with one another. There is in fact often a disjunction between them. Our understanding of myth as one part of life in a way that was unknown to archaic people is one among many indications of the modern separation of religion from the rest of life.

---

[11]See, e.g., Stephen Edelston Toulmin, *An Examination of the Place of Reason in Ethics* (Cambridge: Cambridge University Press, 1960), chaps. 7–8.

Clifford Geertz, in his study of Islam, discusses the religious dimension of human experience and its relation to the rest of life. He defines the religious dimension as involving "the conviction that the values one holds are grounded in the inherent structure of reality, that between the way one ought to live and the way things really are there is an unbreakable inner connection." [12] He terms these two aspects of life "ethos" and "world view" and sees religious symbols as uniting them.

> When men turn to everyday living they see things in everyday terms. If they are religious men, those everyday terms will in some way be influenced by their religious convictions, for it is in the nature of faith, even the most unworldly and least ethical, to claim effective sovereignty over human behavior. The internal fusion of world view and ethos is . . . the heart of the religious perspective, and the job of sacred symbols is to bring about that fusion. [13]

He observes that as religious symbols have lost their power in the modern world what is left is "religious-mindedness" — the religious forms are still followed, but they no longer affect all of the individual's life. The everyday secular world is no longer grounded in the experience of the sacred. For some people it is not even a case of following religious forms that no longer open onto the sacred, but rather a complete disregard for religion's symbols. In both instances we are seeing the process of secularization at work. The term *secular* has been used to describe the world view or fundamental attitude that is characteristic of our time. Langdon Gilkey defines secularity as "the affirmation of life in the world, of our ordinary daily existence among the things and people that make up our immediate environment. Here it is that reality, truth, and value are to be found." [14] The fundamental attitude of our time is one that emphasizes the human rather than the transcendent. People tend to rely on human solutions to problems. They look to technology or to science rather than to supernatural beings to regulate their world. Social institutions are seen to be created by history, geography, and human forces rather than being divinely ordained; and they lack the authority such supernatural ordination would provide. The dominant attitude is that people are on their own in an environment that they have created and that is subject to their control. Gilkey also says:

---

[12]Clifford Geertz, *Islam Observed: Religious Development in Morocco and Indonesia* (Chicago: University of Chicago Press, 1971), p. 97.

[13]Ibid., p. 110.

[14]Langdon Gilkey, *Naming the Whirlwind: The Renewal of God-Language* (Indianapolis: Bobbs-Merrill Company, 1969), p. 250.

Our life, therefore, is not dependent on a sacred order or a transcendent divinity for either its existence or its meaning. Rather, what is *real* in our universe is only the profane, the contingent, blind causes that have produced us, the relative social institutions in which we live, the things and artifacts that we can make, and our relations to one another; any other "sacred" realm of existence partakes for our age more of fantasy than it does of deity. Correspondingly, what we can *know* are only these finite, contingent factors we see around us. That is, valid knowing occurs only where we can directly experience, manipulate, test, and verify; any other "knowing" than such a radically empirical mode of inquiry, for example, by poetic imagination, by religious vision, or even by rational speculation, severs its touch with what is "real" and so in fact tells us more about our own psychological and verbal problems than it does about what there is. And, finally, what is *valuable* is not some far-off heaven, or a mystical union with a transcendent reality, but a better life here and now, among men in this world. [15]

Gilkey is being descriptive when he offers this account of modern human beings. He is not celebrating secularity so much as saying this is where we are. His question is how do we discover that sacred dimension of reality if this is where we begin?

Gilkey gives four characteristics of the secular spirit that shapes modern attitudes toward reality, toward value: contingency, relativity, temporality, and autonomy.[16] Contingency indicates the lack of necessity for anything to be. Things simply *are* rather than being a part of a divine plan. If we discover an apparent orderliness in the world or ourselves, it is simply by accident that it exists. There is no broader understanding we can have of our universe or our lives fulfilling some larger pattern. Relativity stresses the lack of absolutes. Things exist in relation to each other and are conditioned by those relationships. There is nothing we can know absolutely in itself. Temporality is related to this as well. There is nothing we can know that stands outside time. To exist is to be in time and to be in time is to change. The fourth characteristic, autonomy, indicates the freedom and self-sufficiency that belong to those who live in a world with no transhuman authority. Autonomy means both freedom and the responsibility to fashion one's life in a meaningful way. Nothing is given to us; all must be created by us.

We can easily see the positive accomplishments that have grown out of some of these characteristics. Autonomy and relativity, for example, have increased the possibilities for growth and creativity in every area of human thought—science, art,

---

[15]Ibid., pp. 38–39.
[16]Ibid., see pt. 1, chap. 2 and pt. 2, chap. 3.

theology—that were restrained by absolute authorities that limited the possible areas of exploration. So there has certainly been growth in the secular age. But the secular spirit has encountered many brick walls as well. The secular spirit, which prides itself on dealing with the actualities of human experience, continually fails to encompass the full range of actual experience. In regard to relativity Gilkey says:

> A nonsecular dimension in our experience appears in the lived character of secular life, despite the fact that the forms of our modern self-understanding have no capacity for dealing with it. This strange interloper into our secularity appears not so much . . . a presence—though it may be—as a final limit and a demand; not so much an answer as an ultimate question. . . . It has the character of ultimacy, of finality, of the unconditioned which transcends, undergirds, and even threatens our experience of the ordinary passage of things and our dealing with the entities in that passage. It is, therefore, sacred as well as ultimate, the region where value as well as existence is grounded.[17]

About autonomy he says:

> Autonomy has not conquered either the demons of sin or of fate, nor are we free from their corresponding effects of guilt, anxiety and the threat of meaninglessness. Consequently, the ancient religious problems of confidence, repentance, reconciliation, and of hope are as much the deepest problems of a secular age, made up entirely of relative things and autonomous men, as they were in the life of primitive or ancient man, or in the holy world of the Church. . . . Because of this continued relevance, modern man, too, lives by "myths" concerning the origin and eradication of his fault and expressing his faith about his destiny.[18]

Our actual experience in the secular world cannot be contained by the beliefs about reality, truth, and value that secularity proclaims. Within the secular world modern human beings encounter the sacred, even though they may no longer have the religious or sacred symbols that can meaningfully connect the two realms with each other. The discontinuity that is felt between them creates an anxiety that indicates once again the connection between the sacred and the secular that is necessary for the wholeness of life.

RELIGION AND CULTURE IN THE MODERN WORLD

Many theologians in the modern period have sought to deal with the disjunction between religion and the rest of life through an investigation of the relationship between religion and culture. This question takes on special importance in a time when a

[17]Ibid., p. 253.
[18]Ibid., p. 258.

discontinuity between them is felt. It is also at this time that literature, as one expression of culture, becomes of special importance to the study of religion.

Culture may be understood as the expressions and interpretations of a people.[19] The root of culture is sometimes said to be the rational abilities of human beings. It is our reason which develops our culture and makes us by nature cultural animals. Others say that this is too narrow a definition both of human beings and of culture. Ernst Cassirer sees the power of symbolization—which includes conceptual language (reason), but also emotive language—as underlying the cultural activities of human beings.

> Reason is a very inadequate term with which to comprehend the forms of man's cultural life in all their richness and variety. But all these forms are symbolic forms. Hence, instead of defining man as an *animal rationale,* we should define him as an *animal symbolicum.* By so doing we can designate his specific difference, and we can understand the new way open to man—the way to civilization.[20]

Paul Tillich associates culture with the spiritual dimension of human existence, and includes within the spiritual dimension the aesthetic, cognitive, and moral aspects of human behavior.[21] Works of art, the enterprises of reason (science and philosophy, for example), and ethical systems that reflect the values of a people are thus considered by Tillich to comprise their culture. But what about the place of religion in such a schema? Culture is sometimes considered to be the realm of the secular or profane and religion the realm of the sacred. Thus, religion and culture would seem to be two different—and opposing—areas of human existence. To see that this cannot be so simple a dichotomy we need merely look at the aspects of religion that utilize what we have already identified with culture: language and symbols as they are embodied in myth and ritual and scripture; pictorial images—art—which are a part of most religions; theological systems, which employ concepts and reason; ethical prescriptions, which tell the followers of a religion how they should live, what they should value. On the other hand, can we collapse the distinctions between

[19]Giles Gunn, "The Literary Critic in Religious Studies," *The Interpretation of Otherness: Literature, Religion, and the American Imagination* (New York: Oxford University Press, 1979), p. 98.

[20]Ernst Cassirer, *An Essay on Man: An Introduction to a Philosophy of Human Culture* (New Haven: Yale University Press, 1962), p. 26.

[21]Paul Tillich, see chap. 1, "Religion as a Dimension in Man's Spiritual Life," *Theology of Culture,* ed. Robert C. Kimball (New York: Oxford University Press, 1964).

them and say that religion is simply one aspect of culture and that the religious experience we described earlier (the Ultimate, the *Wholly Other,* the *mysterium tremendum et fascinosum)* is defined by the limits of culture, i.e., the creations of the human spirit? This seems contrary to our understanding of religion.

Paul Tillich suggests a different kind of relationship through his phrase, "religion is the substance of culture, culture is the form of religion."[22] Tillich begins his discussion of the religious dimension of human life by questioning whether religion lies within the moral, the cognitive, or the aesthetic spheres. Is it human reason that leads one to God? This is the answer the Deists in the eighteenth century came close to. Is it one's moral nature? Those who would see religion as being equal to good deeds would agree. Liberal theologians of the nineteenth century such as Ritschl moved toward this answer. Is it the aesthetic realm, the human power to create beauty, that brings people to God? This answer has appeared at various times, from both theologians and artists. In the nineteenth century the Romantic movement tended in this direction: poets saw themselves in the role of priests as religion seemed to be losing its place to science.

Tillich says that religion is not to be equated with any of these functions of the human spirit. And these functions, as we have seen, would fall under the category of culture. Nor is there another function we would call "religious" that would stand beside the moral, cognitive, and aesthetic. Rather, religion is "the dimension of depth" in all these functions.

> What does the metaphor *depth* mean? It means that the religious aspect points to that which is ultimate, infinite, unconditional in man's spiritual life. Religion, in the largest and most basic sense of the word, is ultimate concern. And ultimate concern is manifest in all creative functions of the human spirit.[23]

In understanding religion as ultimate concern Tillich is pointing to the "Ground of Being," the transcendent, that which people have called God. All that is human is necessarily non-ultimate. Human beings and their creations are limited. They are finite and are conditioned by the time, place, and circumstances of their creation. The object of one's ultimate concern (God), on the other hand, is unconditional, infinite, and without limits. Tillich points out that all people have an ultimate concern in their lives. There is something to which they would subject everything else, something

[22]Ibid., p. 42.
[23]Ibid., pp. 7–8.

that is valued above all else and that determines what *will* be valued. For some people this might be the nation or material success or one's family. It is possible for a person to see any one of these as having ultimate value. However, we can easily see that none of these is ultimate itself. The nation is finite and limited. It is subject to change and decay. It is open to corruption or to final dissolution. The same is true of the other examples. In other words, it is possible to hold something up as the object of one's ultimate concern which is not in fact ultimate. In Tillich's terms this is idolatry. A truly ultimate concern demands absolute commitment and promises absolute fulfillment. Only that which is truly ultimate can provide this absolute fulfillment.[24] Thus anything finite that claims to be ultimate (including the church) is idolatrous. The finite can, however, point to that which is ultimate as, for example, the symbols of the church are able to do insofar as the church recognizes both its own finitude and the ultimate to which it points. This is possible because the finite is grounded in the ultimate. It takes its meaning, its value, from that which established it and transcends it.

We may now return to Tillich's formulation: "Religion is the substance of culture, culture is the form of religion." Religion understood as ultimate concern is the *substance* of all cultural creations. Without this depth dimension they are meaningless, without foundation, without value. Tillich says that in a perfected world (Eden or the "New Jerusalem," which will be established at the end of time, the eschaton) there would be no separate category in human affairs called religion; there would be no separate institution called the church. He refers to the Revelation of John:

> According to the visionary who has written the last book of the Bible, there will be no temple in the heavenly Jerusalem, for God will be all in all. There will be no secular realm, and for this very reason there will be no religious realm. Religion will be again what it is essentially, the all-determining ground and substance of man's spiritual life.[25]

But as it is, we live as fallen human beings. There is a separation between the essential and existential aspects of our nature, between what we should and could be and what we are. And as long as this is the case, there will be an area of life we call religion.

This area of life, to return to the second half of Tillich's phrase, "culture is the form of religion," must necessarily express

[24]See Tillich, *Dynamics of Faith,* chap. 1.
[25]Tillich, *Theology of Culture,* p. 8.

itself through the forms of culture. The language and symbols and experiences of a certain time and place become the forms through which the ultimate can be apprehended. In a sense, then, the church is a cultural creation. Insofar as it points to that which transcends culture, it is more than a cultural creation. But we have access to the ultimate only through the forms, the symbols of our culture.

An examination of literature from this point of view would begin with the understanding that "there is no cultural creation without an ultimate concern expressed in it."[26] If we are to discover the forms of expression of our culture's ultimate concern, it will be important to examine literary works. In our time it may be that the sacred will confront a person within the secular world in a way that it could not within the setting of the church.

[26]Ibid., p. 42.

Chapter Three
THE ARTIST AND MODERN CULTURE

Just as religion is brought to expression in the forms of its culture, so all artists, existing as they must in a certain time and place, are integrally related to the culture within which and out of which they create. In one sense an artist is the scribe for his or her culture, giving expression to the world view and values of a particular time and place. However, the artist is also often the prophet of the culture, standing on the leading edge and speaking the word that has not yet entered fully into the consciousness of the general society. Because of this possibility we can discover through works of the imagination not only what a culture is, but also what it is in the process of becoming.

In this chapter we will begin by looking at a few general examples of how artists at different periods reveal the distinctiveness of their cultures. We will then examine the development of literature in relation to culture in the modern period. As we concentrate our attention on literature, we will also note corresponding effects on religion. As might be expected, we will find a parallel between this discussion and our previous comments on religion and myth in the modern world. The disjunction we saw between the sacred and the secular is revealed in literature and the other arts as fragmentation of life in its many aspects. Nathan Scott has titled a book on "the theological horizon of modern literature" *The Broken Center*. He takes the title from W. B. Yeats's poem "The Second Coming," which begins:

Things fall apart; the center cannot hold;
Mere anarchy is loosed upon the world.

The assertion of much of modern literature, as well as much of modern life, is that the center has been lost. Whatever once held all of life together in a meaningful whole has somehow lost the power to do so for us. Literature gives voice to this dilemma of modern human beings, often pointing to the absence of and the human longing for the sacred as well as occasional hints of its presence.

ART AND CULTURE

To say that literature reveals what a culture is and what it is coming to be involves more than the "themes" or ideas of a work of literature. We cannot talk about art without talking about both form and content. We must understand the way in which the theme is embodied because this affects the content. There is no work of art without both form and content integrally woven together. We can know the content only as it is embodied in a form; we can recognize form only as it gives shape to content. Thus, in our discussion of literature we must examine these two aspects together, for it is only in this wholeness that they have existence at all. W. B. Yeats describes this mysterious interrelation between form and content in his poem, "Among School Children":

> O chestnut tree, great-rooted blossomer,
> Are you the leaf, the blossom, or the bole?
> O body swayed to music, O brightening glance,
> How can we know the dancer from the dance?

Through the form and content of a work of art, inextricably bound together, we discover a world of values and meaning that is related to the values and meaning of the culture out of which the artist creates.

We find examples of this interrelationship between culture and the wholeness of the artistic creation in the visual arts. We can compare, for example, two paintings, one created by Sebastiano del Piombo called *Christ in Limbo* (ca. 1530), the other by Paul Cezanne, which is a painting of Piombo's painting (1868–70). Even though the subject is the same in these paintings, our response to them is quite different. They reveal to us two diverse cultures with different religious and artistic values. Piombo's painting, done in the period of the High Renaissance in Italy, reveals the importance of classical form, the realism created through careful attention to anatomical exactness, and the use of *chiaroscuro* (light and dark) to achieve depth and unity in the picture. The Christ is clearly central to Piombo's painting. The focus of light in the painting, which emphasizes the divinity of Christ, is the figure of Christ holding a staff whose form is a cross which reaches into the heavens.

Figure 1. Sebastiano del Piombo, *Christ in Limbo*, c. 1530. The Prado, Madrid.

Figure 2. Paul Cezanne, *Christ in Limbo*, 1868–70.

Cezanne's painting of this painting comes from the nineteenth century. Impressionism, with its goal of revealing not the external reality so much as its internal meaning, has had its effect on him. By disregarding the traditional rules of *chiaroscuro* Cezanne collapses depth and surface. There is an immediacy to the painting to which foreground and background are equally present. Christ is still the center of the painting, but there is now more of a sense of Christ involved with the sufferers in Limbo. The staff no longer reaches to heaven; the light is diffused on all the participants. It is the human side of Christ as the suffering servant we experience through this painting.

Through sculptures by August Rodin and Constantin Brancusi and a painting by René Magritte, we can make yet another comparison of artists and their cultures. Rodin's *The Kiss* (1886–98) reveals the influence of the Impressionist movement on sculpture. Although there is a great degree of realism in his work, it is not photographic realism. There is also a sense of unfinishedness to it. The rough-hewn marble out of which the figures emerge holds them firmly to the earth. There is not a spiritualization of the kiss, but a graphic illustration of earthiness—in all of its beauty and tension—in human relationships. In Brancusi's *The Kiss* (1908) we see the influence of Expressionism. In this art there is an emphasis on form; here Brancusi emphasizes the return to primitive form, sculpting out only what is necessary to distinguish two figures. Here there is none of the tension found in Rodin, but a sense of primeval oneness. As a contrast found in the contemporary period we see Magritte's *The Lovers* (1928). Photographic realism is present, but we are shocked out of realism into Surrealism by the unexpected loss of identity of the figures who are distinguishable only by the clothing they wear. The sense of realism is also destroyed by the way the molding on the ceiling abruptly ends. Whereas in Brancusi's sculpture the almost indistinguishable faces indicate primordial unity, in Magritte the identical, covered faces reveal the loss of identity and total separation within the contemporary world, even between "lovers."

This final example reveals that the artist does not necessarily affirm what he or she discovers as the values of the culture. The prophet, traditionally, has spoken to call people back from a disaster they were approaching. Magritte's image of the anonymity in human relationships in our culture may be calling us to acknowledge our facelessness and perhaps even to remove our masks.

Figure 3. August Rodin, *The Kiss*, 1886–98. Musée du Luxembourg.

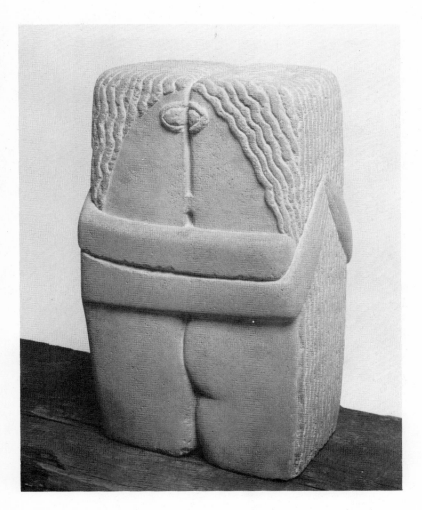

Figure 4. Constantin Brancusi, *The Kiss*, 1908. Philadelphia Museum of Art: The Louise and Walter Arensberg Collection.

Figure 5. René Magritte, *The Lovers*. Zeisler Collection, New York.

The interrelationship between artistic creations and the cultures from which they come is also seen in two poems written in different times and different places. The first is a sonnet by William Shakespeare written at the beginning of the seventeenth century:

When in disgrace with fortune and men's eyes
I all alone beweep my outcast state,
And trouble deaf Heaven with my bootless cries,
And look upon myself and curse my fate,
Wishing me like to one more high in hope,
Featured like him, like him with friends possessed,
Desiring this man's art and that man's scope,
With what I most enjoy contented least —
Yet in these thoughts myself almost despising,
Haply I think on thee, and then my state,
Like to the lark at break of day arising
From sullen earth, sings hymns at heaven's gate.
   For thy sweet love remembered such wealth brings,
   That then I scorn to change my state with kings.

(Sonnet 29)

We are struck immediately by several elements of this poem which are not common to us. The rigid sonnet form itself may seem unusual to us in a time when free verse and lack of rhyme are more common in poetry. The sonnet form, which Shakespeare used and made famous, consists of three quatrains rhyming *abab, cdcd, efef* and a couplet rhyming *gg.* The formalized structure of the poem tells something about the Elizabethan culture out of which it grew, and a study of the culture would enrich our understanding of the poem. It is not only the structure that strikes us as different. The words, images, and symbols of the poem are often foreign to us. We need to be told that "bootless" means vain; "beweep" may sound strange to our ears. The phrase "heaven's gate" is not commonly used in our culture, and it is not likely that we would use the "state of kings" as a superlative vision to reveal how much more important is our love for another person. Nonetheless, we know what Shakespeare is talking about. We do know the state of dejection that is described in the first two quatrains and reaches its nadir in the first line of the third with self-hatred. We also know the importance of another person, the love we share with another, the way love lifts us out of our depression so that no matter how unhappy our state of mind or our position in the world, we are glad to be who we are because, as is revealed in the closing couplet, it is in being who we are that we are loved.

Another culture is revealed in a poem written in 1686 by Basho, perhaps the most famous Japanese haiku poet;

古池や 蛙飛びこむ 水の音

The old pond, ah!
A frog jumps in:
The water's sound!

The first problem we have with this poem is that it is written in Japanese. We have a translation, but one feels with this poetry that it is difficult to capture the image in another language. And it is this *image,* constituting the entire poem, that strikes us immediately. This poem does not have the elaborate form and structured ideas of a Shakespearean sonnet. We are familiar with a pond, a frog, the sound of water. But we may well have trouble seeing this as poetry. We may struggle to figure out what we can say *about* this poem. However, haiku, in its intention, probes to the heart of universal experience, experience that is shared by all people and thus should speak to all people.

The haiku form is rigidly set. It is made up of seventeen syllables in three lines (5-7-5) (not recreated in this translation). Haiku poetry is almost always nature poetry, and it is intimately connected to Zen Buddhism. A study of haiku poetry would be enriched by a study of Zen. Basho says this about haiku:

> Go to the pine if you want to learn about the pine, or to the bamboo if you want to learn about the bamboo. And in doing so, you must leave your subjective preoccupation with yourself. Otherwise you impose yourself on the object and do not learn. Your poetry issues of its own accord when you and the object have become one—when you have plunged deep enough into the object to see something like a hidden glimmering there. However well phrased your poetry may be, if your feeling is not natural—if the object and yourself are separate—then your poetry is not true poetry but merely your subjective counterfeit.[1]

The intention of the haiku poem is to create this moment of union of subject and object, this moment when existence reveals itself in its depths through the everyday world of nature. Paradoxically, we are led to encounter the ordinary, temporal world in its actuality; and, in the moment of this encounter, we experience the unchanging realm of eternity. This occurs in what might be described as a moment of intuition. This is what the poem presents and the way it asks us to respond. This may be difficult for our Western analytic minds, which prefer to play with ideas and to

---

[1]Joan Giroux, *The Haiku Form* (Rutland, Vt.: Charles E. Tuttle Co., 1974) pp. 46–47. Quoting Yuasa Nobuyuki, trans., *Basho: The Narrow Road to the Deep North and other Travel Sketches* (Hammondsworth, Middlesex: Penguin, 1966), p. 33.

reason rather than to be open to intuition. We want to ask what the poem is about; the poem simply wants to be.

Within Basho's poem we see a phenomenon that occurs often in haiku poetry: an internal comparison that, in its juxtaposition, sets off resonating images to create the moment of illumination. In this case it is the silence in which the sound of water is heard as the frog jumps into the pond. The noise serves to accent the eternal silence; it makes it reverberate as we might image the water rippling out in wider and wider circles as the frog disturbs it. But the constancy of the water is only heightened by this movement. By the juxtaposition of the "old pond" and the "sound of water," the unchanging eternal and the particular temporal, we are brought into a unity with the object itself; and we experience the eternal, universal truth contained therein. The image of Basho's poem may also serve as an exemplar of haiku poetry in that the image resonates in us, reaching further and further out into the reaches of being itself.

With both Shakespeare and Basho we are entering into very particular worlds. Their poems were written out of, and are expressions of, cultural situations that are not our own. Yet through these particulars—through looking closely at the jug in the picture, to return to Joyce Cary's image—a door is opened and meaning is revealed to us and for us. This is the power of symbol—and literature is a symbolic form: only through its particularity can we perceive the wholeness in which it participates. And in perceiving this wholeness we are brought to the particular meaning of it for our lives. Through the particular jug we are brought to the jug of jugs; and in astonishment we say, "Yes, jugs are like that!" though we had not known it before.

Through our attention to the wholeness of a work of art, then, we may come to understand the culture out of which it comes. This is not to say, however, that an artistic creation is a simple reflection that serves as a travelogue for viewing another time or our own, a form of history whose truth can be evaluated by comparing it with factual documents. A work of art is a hypothetical creation, a product of the artist's imagination, that has neither obligation nor desire to be true to the "facts" of the culture. But the truth of a time may reside in more than its facts, and through the creation of a fictional world the artist may reveal what the ruling passions of a culture are—what the culture essentially is or what it longs to be. It is at this point that the work of art opens itself to our discussion of its religious possibilities.

THE BEGINNINGS OF MODERN CULTURE

The "modern period" is an ambiguous term whose point of beginning differs depending on the area of culture one examines. Francis Bacon, who wrote about 1600, is sometimes used as the pivotal figure between the medieval and the modern periods in the Western world. Clearly, there was not one moment at which the world ceased being medieval and became modern. It was, rather, a gradual process, occurring in different places at different times, in different fields at different times, often imperceptibly for people living then. But in retrospect it is quite clear that a new period in Western experience blossomed in every area of human thought. We can see signs of the beginnings of this process as early as the fifteenth century with the rise of nation states, the invention of the Gutenberg press that made the printed word available to large numbers of people for the first time, and the Protestant Reformation, which resulted in a new pluralism in Christianity. The beginnings of modern science in the seventeenth century are another sign of the new age. Industrialization and new developments in urban living produced new patterns of socialization. The revolutions of the eighteenth century and the rise of democracy out of the medieval monarchies also indicate what we call the modern period. In the Constitution of the United States we find the idea of the separation of church and state based on the belief that it is possible for people of different religions to live together under one secular government.

In every area we see new freedom for the individual and a new emphasis on individuality. New possibilites for economic position and ways of viewing and exploring the world open up. The medieval synthesis with the church as its focal point, unifying all aspects of life, breaks down. The variety of forms that result lead to new opportunities for creativity; but they also signal an increase in the fragmentation of life and the loss of a center, with which contemporary human beings are still struggling.

The area of culture that has been thought by many people to have the ability to be the center and to overcome the fragmentation of modernism developed in the Rationalism and Empiricism of the seventeenth and eighteenth centuries. The rise of science has had great implications for both religion and literature, and we will focus our attention on this aspect of modernity.

The eighteenth century has been called the "Age of Reason" and the "Enlightenment." The terms indicate the belief in a new kind of clear-sightedness based on logical-mathematical and empirical methods for observing and understanding the world. This resulted on the empirical side, for example, in the materialism of Thomas Hobbes: what is real is what is corporeal.

> The *Universe,* that is, the whole masse of all things that are, is Corporeall, that is to say, Body; and hath the dimensions of Magnitude, namely, Length, Bredth, and Depth: also every part of the Body, is likewise Body, and hath the like dimensions; and consequently every part of the Universe, is Body; and that which is not Body, is no part of the Universe: And because the Universe is All, that which is no part of it, is Nothing; and consequently *no where.*[2]

The other way in which reason exercised its powers was through Rationalism. René Descartes' famous dictum, "Cogito ergo sum," "I think, therefore I am," emphasized a division of mind and body—that which thinks and that which is to be thought. Logic and its useful language of mathematics provide the best tools for dealing with this world.

A common image for the universe, so understood, is that of the machine. Things function according to a preestablished design, and we, through observation and logic, can understand the pattern. The religious understanding that complemented this view of the world was Deism. God was acknowledged to be the master machine builder who set the world in motion and then retired behind the scenes, leaving it to function on its own. Human responsibility to such a God was to seek to understand the machine—reason is the judge of revelation—and in this way to fulfill one's obligation to keep it running smoothly.

In this view of the world, reason and denotative powers of language are stressed. What is real is what can be described. What can be described is what can be observed. For religion, this meant there was little use in seeking out the machine maker behind the machine. To worship God was to observe and reason about the machine. Religion could still be useful as it helped to instill in people the morality that would duplicate in the human realm the orderliness that was observable in the natural realm and thus help to preserve an orderly, cohesive society. Literature would seem to have little use within such a world view. In fact, it was discouraged by many who saw it as being a waste of time because it dealt with unreality and even as serving a negative function because it could lead people into "flights of fancy" away from the realities of the observable world. There were others, though, who saw art as serving a function similar to religion's. It could instruct by revealing

---

[2]Thomas Hobbes, *Leviathan,* chap. 46, cited by Nathan A. Scott, Jr., *Modern Literature and the Religious Frontier* (New York: Harper & Row, 1958), p. 6.

to people the proper way to act. Samuel Johnson, using Aristotle's idea of art as "holding a mirror up to nature," saw the role of the artist as the observer of the "living world" and the revealer through art of the order that is "natural" to human beings but which is often distorted in actual human affairs.[3] The artist must, then, be selective in his observation and must reveal the

> highest and purest that humanity can reach. . . . It is therefore to be steadily inculcated that virtue is the highest proof of understanding, and the only solid basis of greatness; and that vice is the natural consequence of narrow thoughts; that it begins in mistake, and ends in ignominy.[4]

The Neoclassical literature that sought to imitate the orderliness of nature emphasized reasonableness, clarity, and straightforwardness. "Wit" was a term used to describe the highest virtue of literature. John Dryden defined wit as "a propriety of thoughts and words; or, in other terms, thought and words elegantly adapted to the subject."[5] Propriety or decorum, the rightness of language and subject, was stressed. But even so, such use of language was questionable to men such as Hobbes. This emotive language, he said, "though it may 'please and delight our selves, and others,' is incapable of giving a responsible version of experience."[6] The range of poetic experience is thus very limited in this period: to instruct, to please, but always with the decorum, the properness, of a style that knows its limitations well.

An example of the poetry from this period is Alexander Pope's "Essay on Man." Pope uses the formal heroic couplet—iambic pentameter with each two lines rhyming with each other. He describes the state of human beings in their position midway up the "great chain of being." They are part of an orderly organization of being that proceeds from the smallest forms of life to God; and they must fill this position, neither falling below it by ceasing to reason, nor trying to rise above it by seeking to use their reason to understand God. Within the formal boundaries and tone of the Neoclassical style, Pope conveys with great energy and delight this human creature in all its strengths and foibles.

---

[3]Samuel Johnson, "On Fiction," *The Rambler,* no. 4 (1750), reproduced in *The Rambler,* the Yale Edition of the Works of Samuel Johnson, vol. 3, eds. W. J. Bate and Albrecht B. Strauss (New Haven: Yale University Press, 1969), 1:19.

[4]Ibid., pp. 24–25.

[5]John Dryden, "The Author's Apology for Heroic Poetry and Heroic License," prefixed to *State of Innocence,* reproduced in *Literary Criticism of John Dryden,* ed. Arthur C. Kirsch (Lincoln: University of Nebraska Press, 1966), p. 113.

[6]Hobbes cited by Scott, *Modern Literature,* p. 8.

The bliss of man (could Pride that blessing find)
Is not to act or think beyond mankind;
No powers of body or of soul to share,
But what his nature and his state can bear.
Why has not Man a microscopic eye?
For this plain reason, Man is not a Fly.
Say what the use, were finer optics given,
T' inspect a mite, not comprehend the heaven?
Or touch, if tremblingly alive all o'er,
To smart and agonize at every pore?
Or quick effluvia darting through the brain,
Die of a rose in aromatic pain?
If nature thundered in his opening ears,
And stunned him with the music of the spheres,
How would he wish that Heaven had left him still
The whispering Zephyr, and the purling rill?
Who finds not Providence all good and wise,
Alike in what it gives, and what denies?[7]

Human powers of reason are limited, and to attempt to overcome this limitation is to defy the order that includes all creation. What is open to human reason is the world we can observe. It is the role of human beings to serve God by fulfilling their position:

Know then thyself, presume not God to scan;
The proper study of Mankind is Man.[8]

THE ROMANTIC REACTION

By the end of the eighteenth century and through much of the nineteenth century, a reaction took place against this tendency to emphasize reason in all aspects of life and its counterpart, wit, as the highest ideal of poetry. The Romantic poets and theorists emphasized emotion more than reason, the imagination rather than wit, and an organic rather than mechanical view of both literature and the world. William Wordsworth describes poetry as the "spontaneous overflow of powerful feelings."[9] Although he adds that our feelings are modified and directed by thinking long and deeply (emotion recollected in tranquillity), the source of poetic

---

[7]Alexander Pope, "An Essay on Man," Epistle 1, lines 189–206, reproduced in *Alexander Pope: Selected Poetry and Prose,* ed. William K. Wimsatt, Jr. (New York: Holt, Reinhart and Winston, 1951), pp. 134–35.

[8]Ibid., Epistle 2, lines 1–2, p. 138.

[9]William Wordsworth, Preface to *Lyrical Ballads,* 2nd ed. (1802), reproduced in *Literary Criticism of William Wordsworth,* ed. Paul M. Zall (Lincoln: University of Nebraska Press, 1966), p. 42.

inspiration cannot be contained by reason or wit. Wordsworth speaks out against poetic diction — the prescribed formality of the Neoclassical era — and asserts that the language of poetry must be the language of common speech. It is not contrived but develops organically from the poet's imagination.

Although the Romantics reacted against the Neoclassical conventions, this does not mean they disregarded form. Samuel Taylor Coleridge says,

> The spirit of poetry, like all other living powers, must of necessity circumscribe itself by rules, were it only to unite power with beauty. It must embody in order to reveal itself; but a living body is of necessity an organized one, — and what is organization, but the connection of parts to a whole, so that each part is at once end and means![10]

He goes on to stress that one must not confuse "mechanical regularity with organic form. . . . The organic form . . . is innate; it shapes as it develops itself from within."[11]

The importance of the poet and the creative power of the imagination are stressed in Romantic theory. The materialism of Hobbes emphasized human perception as purely reception of stimuli from the external world. For the Romantics, something new was created by the power of the imagination and that something new was not subject to the analysis of either empiricism or rationalism. According to Percy Bysshe Shelley, the poet has both a creative and a synthetic function.

> The functions of the poetical faculty are twofold: by one it creates new materials of knowledge, and power, and pleasure; by the other it engenders in the mind a desire to reproduce and arrange them according to a certain rhythm and order, which may be called the beautiful and the good.[12]

Coleridge describes the poet in this way:

> What is poetry? is so nearly the same question with, what is a poet? that the answer to the one is involved in the solution of the other. For it is a distinction resulting from the poetic genius itself, which sustains and modifies the images, thoughts, and emotions of the poet's own mind.
>
> The poet, described in *ideal* perfection, brings the whole soul of man into activity, with the subordination of its faculties to each other, according to their relative worth and dignity. He diffuses a tone and spirit of unity, that blends, and (as it were) *fuses*, each into each, by that synthetic and

---

[10]Samuel Taylor Coleridge, *Shakespearean Criticism*, 2 vols., ed. Thomas Middleton Raysor (London: J. M. Dent & Sons, 1964), 1:197.

[11]Ibid., p. 198.

[12]Percy Bysshe Shelley, *A Defense of Poetry,* reproduced in *Shelley's Prose or The Trumpet of a Prophecy*, ed. David Lee Clark (Albuquerque: University of New Mexico Press, 1954), p. 293.

magical power, to which we have exclusively appropriated the name of imagination. This power . . . reveals itself in the balance or reconciliation of opposite or discordant qualities.[13]

Wordsworth says of the poet that he is "a man . . . endued with more lively sensibility, more enthusiasm and tenderness, who has a greater knowledge of human nature, and a more comprehensive soul, then are supposed to be common among mankind."[14] The Romantic poets saw themselves as possessing a sensitivity that opened a special understanding to them, which they could share with others through poetry.

Many of the Romantics discussed the relationship of their work to that of science. There was an awareness of a conflict existing between them, and there was an attempt to assert the worth of poetry as a human enterprise. It was not just "flights of fancy" or the decorous turn of phrase. It had a validity of its own, not subject to the criteria of science. Wordsworth does not discount science as an avenue of knowledge, but he does assert that science does not have the only claim to knowledge.

> The knowledge both of the Poet and the Man of Science is pleasure; but the knowledge of the one cleaves to us as a necessary part of our existence, our natural and unalienable inheritance; the other is a personal and individual acquisition, slow to come to us, and by no habitual and direct sympathy connecting us with our fellow-beings. The Man of Science seeks truth as a remote and unknown benefactor; he cherishes and loves it in his solitude: the Poet, singing a song in which all human beings join with him, rejoices in the presence of truth as our visible friend and hourly companion. Poetry is the breath and finer spirit of all knowledge; it is the impassioned expression which is in the countenance of all Science. . . . The Poet binds together by passion and knowledge the vast empire of human society, as it is spread over the whole earth, and over all time. . . . Poetry is the first and last of all knowledge—it is as immortal as the heart of man.[15]

Poetry is, in fact, a *superior* form of knowledge because it can unite all humanity and all human endeavors. In its organic form it imitates and participates in the organic form of the reality that shapes the universe. In this understanding the poet is close to taking on the role of the creator and poetic activity does become an analogue to divine creativity. It is because of a correspondence between things earthly and things divine that the poet is able through his creations to reveal eternal truth.

[13]Samuel Taylor Coleridge, *Biographia Literaria*, chap. 14, reproduced in *Selected Poetry and Prose of Coleridge*, ed. Donald A. Stauffer (New York: Random House, 1951), pp. 268–69.
[14]Wordsworth, Preface to *Lyrical Ballads*, p. 48.
[15]Ibid., p. 52.

In Shelley's writings we see this association of religion and poetry, the priest and the poet, made most explicit. He enlarges the definition of the poet to include all those who are able to perceive and express through the imagination the eternal order lying within the world. These people, these poets, "who imagine and express this indestructible order . . . draw into a certain propinquity with the beautiful and the true that partial apprehension of the agencies of the invisible world which is called religion."[16] He goes on to associate both the poet and poetry with the transcendent:

> A poet participates in the eternal, the infinite, and the one. . . . A poem is the very image of life expressed in its eternal truth. . . . Poetry is indeed something divine. It is at once the center and circumference of knowledge; it is that which comprehends all science and that to which all science must be referred.[17]

In its effort to reestablish the importance of the poetic endeavor against the claims of rationalism and Hobbesian empiricism to convey all truth, Romanticism elevated poetic knowledge to the highest of human achievements and the point at which the human and the divine come together. Wordsworth uses the imagery of religion—soul, prophecy, priestly, spirit, holy services—as he describes an act of poetic creation in his long poem *The Prelude*. He reveals the workings of the imagination as it creates in harmony with the natural world and the transcendent.

> Thus far, O Friend! did I, not used to make
> A present joy the matter of a song,
> Pour forth that day my soul in measured strains
> That would not be forgotten, and are here
> Recorded: to the open fields I told
> A prophecy: poetic numbers came
> Spontaneously to clothe in priestly robe
> A renovated spirit singled out,
> Such hope was mine, for holy services.
> My own voice cheered me, and, far more, the mind's
> Internal echo of the imperfect sound;
> To both I listened, drawing from them both
> A cheerful confidence in things to come.
>
> (Book I, lines 46–58)

Wordsworth uses, as do many of the Romantics, the child as the image of a natural piety and knowledge that is lost in maturity and can only be regained through poetic reflection. In "My Heart Leaps Up" he says,

[16]Shelley, *Defense of Poetry,* p. 279.
[17]Ibid., pp. 279, 281, 293.

The Child is father of the Man;
And I could wish my days to be
Bound each to each by natural piety.

And in "Ode: Intimations of Immortality," he describes the child as "Nature's Priest" and "Mighty Prophet! Seer blest!" What the child possesses by nature the adult can regain only through poetic contemplation. This tendency again reveals a revolt against reason, an affirmation of the natural, the innate wisdom that is present before the development of the powers of reason and that must undergird them if they are to have any meaning. This wisdom is best revealed in poetry.

COMTE AND ARNOLD

At the same time Wordsworth was writing, another direction was being pursued by the French philosopher, Auguste Comte. Comte was developing what he called a "positive philosophy." His approach was empirical: no statement is worthy of belief, or true, unless it can be verified by the methods of empirical science. Comte saw human history as progressing through three stages: the theological, the metaphysical, and the positive. He saw beginnings of the movement to the positive stage with Francis Bacon, but only in Comte's time were all of the sciences coming to this point. He describes the positive stage in this way:

> In the final, the positive state, the mind has given over the vain search after Absolute notions, the origin and destination of the universe, and the causes of phenomena, and applies itself to the study of their laws, — that is, their invariable relations of succession and resemblance. Reasoning and observation, duly combined, are the means of this knowledge. What is now understood when we speak of an explanation of facts is simply the establishment of a connection between single phenomena and some general facts, the number of which continually diminishes with the progress of science. [18]

The sciences he lists are astronomy, physics, chemistry, and physiology. It is his task to bring social science to the positive stage the others have reached. All knowledge can be contained in these divisions and can be established by empirical means. Literature and religion are not mentioned because they belong to a previous age. In talking about the importance of regenerating education he says, "The best minds are agreed that our European education, still

[18] *The Positive Philosophy of Auguste Comte*, trans. Harriet Martineau, vol. 1, chap. 1, reproduced by Henry D. Aiken in *The Age of Ideology* (New York: The New American Library of World Literature, 1956), p. 125.

essentially theological, metaphysical, and literary, must be superseded by a Positive training, conformable to our time and needs."[19]

Comte developed his system along evolutionary lines and in his later work does make a place for the science of ethics as being useful for this evolution. This science becomes the basis for his "religion of humanity." But throughout his work he insists that the question that must be asked is not "why?" but "how?" and the only meaningful answers that can be given can be verified by empirical science.

Matthew Arnold wrote in the period following Wordsworth and Comte. Although Comte's approach was different from that of Hobbes, it joined with his in reinforcing the elevation of science as the integrating force in society and the diminution of the relevance of literature and religion. Arnold spoke out against the tendency to devalue literature and did so by joining those who saw the decline of religion as inevitable. He made explicit what had been hinted at in the Romantics as he saw literature taking the place of religion and providing the center for all human activities, including sciences. In his criticism of the prevailing scientific emphasis, Arnold was more aware than the Romantics had been of the dangers of the machine age, with its tendency to view technology as the source of human good and the means of achieving it. He saw the humanistic values he proclaimed being pushed aside by the values of an industrial society.

In a time when the "center does not hold"—the religious center of the past has lost its force and those who would hope to make science the new center have not succeeded—Arnold offers "culture" as providing the new integrative power for life. Culture is aptly suited for this task because "it is possessed by the scientific passion as well as by the passion of doing good; . . . it demands worthy notions of reason and the will of God."[20] It believes in the study and actualization of *perfection,* which is the ideal of human beings. Religion also seeks perfection, but culture is superior to religion because it listens to *all* the voices of human experience. Religion, which he identifies as "morality touched by emotion," is good at providing the correct basis of conduct, but it cannot provide the model of beauty, which is equally necessary for perfection. He says of poets, "their ideal of beauty, of sweetness and light, and a human nature complete on all its sides, remains the true ideal of

[19]Ibid., pp. 134–35.
[20]Matthew Arnold, "Sweetness and Light," *Four Essays on Life and Letters,* ed. E. K. Brown (New York: Appleton-Century-Crofts, 1947), p. 36.

perfection still; just as the Puritan's ideal of perfection remains narrow and inadequate."[21] He believes that religion has lost the power it once possessed because of scientific knowledge and historical knowledge, which question the foundations of the Christian tradition. For example, Darwin's theory of evolution seemed to question the scientific validity of the Genesis creation story. But poetry, bound to neither scientific nor historical facts, is prepared to fill this void.

> The future of poetry is immense, because in poetry, where it is worthy of its high destinies, our race, as time goes on, will find an ever surer and surer stay. There is not a creed which is not shaken, not an accredited dogma which is not shown to be questionable, not a received tradition which does not threaten to dissolve. Our religion has materialized itself in the fact, in the supposed fact; it has attached its emotion to the fact, and now the fact is failing it. But for poetry the idea is everything; the rest is a world of illusion, of divine illusion. Poetry attaches its emotion to the idea; the idea *is* the fact. The strongest part of our religion today is its unconscious poetry.[22]

The poetry that will accomplish this must follow the laws of poetic truth and beauty. It must have the "high seriousness" that comes from "absolute sincerity." Along with this excellence of poetic beauty comes the fulfillment of poetry's aim: "Poetry is at bottom a criticism of life; . . . the greatness of a poet lies in his powerful and beautiful application of ideas to life—to the question: How to live."[23] Rather than dismissing the literature from the educational process as Comte would have us do, Arnold would have the study of literature become both the foundation and the fulfillment of education. By incorporating knowledge, beauty, morality, and feeling and by having the power to *synthesize* these different aspects (as for the Romantics), poetry does what science cannot do and what by nature, human beings require. Science gives knowledge, facts, even general conceptions of the universe.

> But still it will be knowledge only which they give us; knowledge not put for us into relation with our sense for conduct, our sense for beauty, and touched with emotion by being so put; not thus put for us, and therefore, to the majority of mankind, after a certain while unsatisfying, wearying.[24]

Comte had found the religious tradition of his time wanting and had sought to establish a new foundation for integrating human

[21]Ibid., p. 48.

[22]Arnold, "The Study of Poetry," ibid., p. 62.

[23]Matthew Arnold, "Wordsworth," reproduced in *Selected Criticism of Matthew Arnold,* ed. Christopher Ricks (New York: New American Library, 1972), p. 375.

[24]Arnold, "Literature and Science," *Four Essays,* p. 107–8.

existence through positivism. Arnold, while rejecting the traditional form of religion, hoped to secure a place for the side of human experience that is not open to empirical analysis through the establishment of "Culture," by which he came to mean literature, as the foundation of all human endeavors and the conveyor of tradition. His hopes for poetry—and for the progressive movement of human beings toward the perfection he felt poetry promised—were immense.

> More and more mankind will discover that we have to turn to poetry to interpret life for us, to console us, to sustain us. Without poetry, our science will appear incomplete; and most of what now passes with us for religion and philosophy will be replaced by poetry.[25]

THE TWENTIETH CENTURY

In part two, "Four Approaches to Religion and Literature," we will see how this discussion is carried on in the twentieth century. We will discover that the center has still not been found. In fact, fragmentation has increased both in the lives of individuals and in the culture as a whole. There is still a tension between art and science, with religion often receiving the same criticism literature does from the positivist critics. Generally, views of art no longer share the optimism of the Romantics and Arnold. Art may still be seen as a possible way of "salvation," but the terms of salvation are more severely limited.

Science, through evolutionary theories and technological advances, encouraged, in the nineteenth and early twentieth centuries, a view of society that was dominated by the idea of "progress." This was a view that the Romantics and Victorians shared. Both saw the human enterprise as advancing, whether through humane letters or technology, toward a point of perfection in which the social order would be dominated by peace and prosperity. There was also a belief that science, continuing the progress begun with Bacon, would yield all the knowledge of the physical world necessary to control it and make it amenable to this perfected human existence. We see this view in social Darwinians such as Spenser, in social philosophers such as Marx, and in literary theorists such as Arnold and the Transcendentalists in America. It is seen in Christian theology in the movement known as Liberalism. With an emphasis on the life and teachings of Jesus—on morality—there was the belief that the Kingdom could be realized within this world.

---

[25]Arnold, "The Study of Poetry," ibid., p. 63.

The hopes that flourished in the nineteenth century, replacing the certainties of the medieval order, have largely disappeared. In psychology, Freud's revelations of the dark, irrational, unconscious side of human nature have called into question the optimism of those who saw a harmonious human order developing either through the cultivation of human reason or human emotion. Socially, we have seen that neither democracy nor technology has transformed the world. Two world wars and two major "police actions" by the United States have not created a world at peace. We have seen, in this "age of humanism," incredible acts of inhumanity perpetrated by one people on another, most obviously the atrocities of the Nazis. In the light of such circumstances, one can speak of "progress" only with bitter irony. Technology has not only failed to provide the basic necessities of life, but it has created the ironic situation of threatening existence by thermal, nuclear, air, and water pollution.

In the area of science, Einstein's theories of relativity and Heisenberg's principle of indeterminancy have made clear that the certainty we thought we could count on from science is simply an illusion. In both the macrocosm and the microcosm we see things in the way we do because of the position in which we stand in relation to them. Scientific theories can be applied only within certain specified situations of relation.

All of these developments have not, of course, been negative. The twentieth century has been a time of immense creativity. But where do we find our center in this world? What provides the focus of life that myth and religion provided in the past? This is the setting in which we will discuss religious dimensions of literature. Through four angles of vision we will search for ways of talking about religion and literature, and through literary and theological materials from the twentieth century we will explore manifestations of religion in our culture.

Part Two
FOUR APPROACHES TO
RELIGION AND LITERATURE

Chapter Four
RELIGIOUS THEMES IN LITERATURE

The first approach to the relationship between religion and literature explores the use of religious symbols and themes in literature. Critics who take this approach usually look at literature that deals with a religious subject, such as Graham Greene's *The Power and the Glory* or T. S. Eliot's "Ash Wednesday." Or they may talk about literature that has a secular subject, but uses religious symbols, such as Faulkner's "The Bear," in which Isaac McCaslin takes up the profession of carpentry because it was the occupation of Jesus of Nazareth; or Ken Kesey's *One Flew Over the Cuckoo's Nest* in which McMurphy is tied down for electroshock therapy with his arms spread out as on a cross and the conduits attached to his head as a crown of thorns. The critic may also take a broader view and discuss literature that may not intentionally use symbols from a religious tradition but may involve themes that are shared by a specific religious tradition. For example, the struggle with the question of the meaning of history in Ralph Ellison's *Invisible Man* might be discussed in light of the Judeo-Christian understanding of history.

The critic using this approach—or any approach for that matter—must be aware of the danger of imposing a structure on a work of art rather than looking closely at what is revealed through the work itself. Sallie TeSelle (McFague), in her book *Literature and the Christian Life,* describes two ways of approaching the relationship between religion and literature that fail to look closely at the work itself. She calls them "amiability" and "discrimination."[1] The first understanding stresses the close relationship

[1]Sallie TeSelle (McFague), *Literature and the Christian Life* (New Haven: Yale University Press, 1966), "amiability," pp. 8–17, "discrimination," pp. 18–33.

between religion and culture. Every work of literature is "crypto-religious" because religion and culture are really just two sides of the same coin. Although Christian doctrine when understood and applied with care can be said to substantiate this view (all finite things take their life from the infinite), the result for the study of religious dimensions of literature has often been unfortunate for both religion and literature. Religion, and especially a specific religious tradition, can be short-changed because the uniqueness of a tradition is lost—literature is made into religion. On the other hand, literature suffers because it has no choice but to be religious. The particularity of the work of art is lost as it becomes an exemplification of, for instance, the Christian tradition. Amiability allows for a mutual conversation between religion and culture, but a conversation in which the uniqueness of what each has to say is lost.

Discrimination, on the other hand, stresses the distinctions between religion and culture. In this case it is most obviously literature that loses out for it must stand under the judgment not of literary catagories but of religious or theological criteria. It must conform as best it is able to the symbols and beliefs of a tradition, but it must always fall short and so come under the judgment of the tradition, as all culture does. Good art will be art that comes closest to portraying the human situation in the terms of a specific religious tradition. This view does not allow literature to offer something of value on its own terms. It is because of this that religion may also suffer from this approach. Literature, if it is allowed to be literature, may provide insights into the human situation that will enrich the theologian's understanding of the human search for meaning that is fulfilled by the transcendent side of the divine-human relationship, which is the subject of theology, not of literature.

R. W. B. Lewis provides us with an image that can serve very effectively to remind us of the dangers of not letting literature be literature and theology, theology. He tells this story about Ralph Waldo Emerson:

> We may perhaps recall the remark made to Emerson by an old Boston lady who, talking about the extreme religious sensibility of an earlier generation, said about those pious folk that "they had to hold on hard to the huckleberry bushes to hinder themselves from being translated." Their instinct was as sound as their impulse was proper.[2]

[2] R. W. B. Lewis, "Hold on Hard to the Huckleberry Bushes," *Trials of the Word* (New Haven: Yale University Press, 1965), p. 97.

The "huckleberry bushes" in Lewis's story are for us the unique particulars of a work of art. We must not be too quick to "translate" ourselves into the region of transcendence beyond them. Lewis goes on to state the problem in this way:

> This issue is whether one scrutinizes literature for its univocal formulations of particular historical doctrines one cherishes or whether one submits for a while to the actual ingredients and the inner movement and growth of a work to see what attitude and insight, including religious attitude and insight, the work itself brings into being.[3]

This advice is important to the creation of a work of art as well as to the critic if a work is to deal fully and successfully with its materials and subject, which grow out of experiences in this world. Art that translates itself into the realm of the transcendent loses the ability to point us in that direction for it is the nature of that experience to be beyond human speech.

Religious experience, in order to be communicated and understood through language, must be symbolic. It is also the nature of literary works to use symbolic forms. Before looking at three specific religious symbols and their expression in literature, we will discuss symbolic language itself. Although religion and literature have always involved symbolic expression, this approach to them becomes especially important in contemporary thought.

RELIGIOUS SYMBOLS AND RELIGIOUS LANGUAGE

Although all language is symbolic, the symbols to be discussed in this chapter in terms of religion and literature can be distinguished from symbols used in such symbol systems as science and logic. One way of differentiating approaches to symbolic language is given by Kenneth Burke's terms, "scientistic" and "dramatistic."[4] The first emphasizes language as definition; the second, language as act. Burke points out that the categories overlap; to define something is an action. But the basic intention of these two approaches to language is different, and each can be useful under certain conditions. Burke's definition of dramatism is "a technique of analysis of language and thought as basically modes of action rather than as means of conveying information."[5] The implications of this include seeing language as involving a process of relationships rather than as statically standing for one

---

[3]Ibid., p. 99.

[4]Kenneth Burke, *Language as Symbolic Action* (Berkeley and Los Angeles: University of California Press, 1966), p. 44.

[5]Ibid., p. 54 citing Webster's *Third New International Dictionary*.

thing. Such a view would emphasize the way words affect other words—the importance of context. It would also stress the multiple possibilities for the meanings of words—their multivalence—rather than their "one-for-one" or univocal quality, which would be important in scientistic analysis. Symbolic language as we shall talk about it in relation to literature and religion is clearly closer to the understanding of language as act. When we refer to symbols, we will be talking not about all language as symbolic, but about this "word-event" character that a certain use of language involves.

Paul Tillich distinguishes these different uses of language by the terms "sign" and "symbol." He says that both symbols and signs point beyond themselves to something else. But a symbol differs from a sign in that "it participates in that to which it points."[6] He uses a stop sign as an example. It conveys information to us (as does Burke's scientistic language), but we could equally well use another sign to convey the same information (e.g., a red light). Language that has the primary intention of conveying information operates in the same way. If we do not know what is meant when someone points out a specimen in a glass case and says, "That is an arachnid," our informer could say instead, "That is a spider," and we would have received the same information.

The example Tillich gives of symbol illustrates its difference from a sign. The flag of a country points to something beyond itself, but it also participates in that to which it points. You could not just as well raise the Hammer and Sickle over the U. S. Capitol as the Stars and Stripes. Nor could a new Betsy Ross come up with a more attractive flag and suggest it should become the new emblem for our country. We see how the flag participates in what it points to (the United States of America) by noting the anger that is aroused by burning a U. S. flag or wearing it as a shirt. It is only because the Stars and Stripes in a symbolic sense *are* America that such actions are taken and such a response is generated.

In terms of a language, an example of the noninterchangeability of a symbol as opposed to a sign is seen in a poem by William Carlos Williams:

---

[6]Paul Tillich, *Dynamics of Faith* (New York: Harper & Row, 1958), p. 42.

so much depends
upon

a red wheel
barrow

glazed with rain
water

beside the white
chickens[7]

Williams creates a significant image for us, an image of the wheelbarrow and the rain water and the chickens, that we cannot reconstruct through paraphrase. In the experience of the poem, we recognize the importance of the three elements he describes (so much depends upon . . .) and the image comes alive for us. We cannot say, this poem is about . . . and then do away with the poem. We *could* say, this stop sign tells us to stop and then forget the sign itself.

Paul Ricoeur describes the complicated workings of a symbol in this way:

> The symbol conceals in its aim a double intentionality. . . . Contrary to perfectly transparent technical signs, which say only what they want to say in positing that which they signify, symbolic signs are opaque, because the first, literal, obvious meaning itself points analogically to a second meaning which is not given otherwise than in it. . . . This opacity constitutes the depth of the symbol, which . . . is inexhaustible.[8]

We could use other terms to describe the literal meaning of Williams's poem. It is the second, analogical, meaning in Ricoeur's terms that we cannot paraphrase, that "is not given otherwise than in it." Ricoeur says that, unlike some analogies, the analogous character of a symbol cannot be considered from *outside*. We must "participate in the latent meaning and thus [we are assimilated] to that which is symbolized without our being able to master the similitude intellectually."[9] We *can* talk about the experience of participating in and being assimilated by the symbol (the poem),

---

[7]William Carlos Williams, "Spring and All," 21, *The Complete Collected Poems of William Carlos Williams, 1906–1938* (Norfolk, Conn.: New Directions, 1938), p. 127.

[8]Paul Ricoeur, *The Symbolism of Evil*, trans. Emerson Buchanan (New York: Harper & Row, 1967), p. 15.

[9]Ibid., p. 16.

for as Ricoeur says, "the symbol gives rise to thought,"[10] but we cannot fully account intellectually for the way that process occurs—the movement from the primary, literal meaning to the latent, inexhaustible meaning.

Although different terms can be used to describe the two functions of language we are here calling sign and symbol, we see clearly that there is a difference in the way we use words. Ricoeur explains it in this way:

> Signification, by its very structure, makes possible at the same time both total formalization—that is to say, the reduction of signs to "characters" and finally to elements of a calculus—*and* the restoration of a full language, heavy with implicit intentionalities and analogical references to something else, which it presents enigmatically.[11]

The use of language we will talk about in terms of religion and literature will be the language that is "heavy with implicit intentionalities," that is "opaque," that cannot be paraphrased without remainder. Although the language of "technical signs" is essential to our life in the world, so is the language of symbols.

In both Tillich's and Ricoeur's understanding of symbol we are referred back to Burke's idea of symbol as involving action. Tillich says that the symbol participates in that to which it points and Ricoeur says that we participate in the symbol. In both cases the participation involves an action. There is not a passivity on the part of either the symbol or the subject for whom the symbol has meaning. Something occurs; there is a word-event. It is this characteristic of the symbol that empowers it to open new dimensions of reality to us, as Tillich says, and new dimensions of ourselves. A transformation occurs through the power of symbolic language as it reveals what cannot be known in any other way.

We should note one thing further about this power of symbols. Tillich points out that a symbol cannot be created or invented. That is, I cannot make a certain word or image have symbolic value for you. The President cannot say tomorrow, the Stars and Stripes are no longer a symbol for America. The church cannot announce that the cross will no longer be a symbol for Christianity. A symbol is born and grows out of the needs of a people. When it no longer serves its symbolic function of opening and transforming—the analogous function described by Ricoeur—it dies.

---

[10]Ibid., "Conclusion: The Symbol Gives Rise to Thought," *passim.*
[11]Ibid., pp. 17–18.

The Special Character of Religious Symbols

Tillich says that faith has no other language than symbols. And he adds immediately, "One should never say 'only a symbol,' but one should say 'not less than a symbol.'"[12] Since the object of religious experience is more than finite, is always transcendent, what finite words could adequately describe this power? The realm of the ultimate can only be spoken of by finite beings through symbols that point to the ultimate and, by participating in that to which they point, open the possibility for transformation. The word "God" is, then, a symbol for the ultimate, which can never be described in finite terms. "God transcends his own name."[13] But through the power of the symbol, that which is transcendent is given concrete expression.

Religious symbols share with all symbols the power of signification; and, unlike signs, they participate in what they point to and draw us into participation with the symbol. Religious symbols differ from other symbols in that what they point to and participate in is the ultimate.

Religious Symbols in Literature

Religious symbols can be used in literature in two ways. One may refer directly to the symbols of a particular tradition: calling someone Christ-like, for example, or naming a character Moses or referring to bread and wine as symbols of communion or of an impending sacrificial death. One may also use these symbols more obliquely: describing a character in a way that one who is familiar with the Christian tradition, for example, would readily understand to be Christ-like. In addition, the critic of a literary work might use symbols from a religious tradition as a way of talking about the work. What we must keep in mind as we explore symbols in any of these ways is that religion and literature are two different things. Religious symbols may be used in a work of literature *hypothetically* to point to what might imaginatively be seen as ultimate. In religion those same symbols may take on the power of ultimate transformation in a life where they are entertained not imaginally but with the commitment of one's whole being. Literature may portray such a commitment, but it is an imaginative portrayal. Thus we must not make literature into religion. On the other

---

[12]Tillich, *Dynamics of Faith,* p.45.
[13]Ibid., pp. 44–45.

hand, we must not flatten out the possibilities of literature by making it conform, image for image, to a religious symbol system. We must not turn a work of art into an allegory so that each stage of development represents a parallel progression in the life of Christ or a theological dogma of the church. Symbols are multivalent; they speak with many voices, at many levels. We cannot rob literary symbols of their power by making this character *equal* Christ or this misfortune *equal* the Fall. With symbols, unlike signs, there are no "equals." There is symbolic action that is never univocal but always creative of a movement that is "heavy with implicit intentionalities."

In the following sections we will discuss several specific religious themes and symbols: the Incarnation, the Fall, and historical and cyclical time. We will look at these themes and the symbols associated with them as they appear in works of literature. We will also see how they can be used to talk about the structure of a work of art and its relationship to the religious tradition out of which the symbols come. We will use examples of literature from the twentieth century and we will see how the traditional symbols of Christianity, for example, take form within the particularities of our culture.[14]

THE INCARNATION

Incarnation means embodiment, the taking on of bodily form. In Christianity this term is used to refer to Jesus Christ as the embodiment of God in human form. Because God chose this way to reveal himself, Christians believe that the world, in all its concreteness, is affirmed. It is not just the spirit of human beings that Christ came to save, but the whole person. There is a judgment made on the world as well, but it is a judgment that leads to salvation. The way of Christianity has not been to reject the physical (material) world as evil and assert the spiritual as good. This dualism is the way of the gnostics and other groups who were early declared heretics by the church. Both the body and the spirit are in need of salvation; and the doctrine of the Incarnation reveals the possibility of this occurring through the life, death, and resurrection of Jesus Christ.

---

[14]This approach to religion and literature is certainly not limited to the Christian or Jewish religious traditions. The religious themes discussed here have manifestations in other religious traditions (e.g., the incarnation is expressed in the image of the *avatar* in Hinduism and the *bodhisattva* in Buddhism). In addition, the dominant religious symbols of other traditions might well suggest other themes to explore in literature.

The meaning of these events is celebrated and reenacted in Christianity through the sacrament of the Eucharist. A sacrament is defined within Christianity as "an outward and visible sign of an inward and spiritual grace." Nathan Scott describes the "sacramental principle" in this way:

> Certain objects or actions or words or places belonging to the ordinary spheres of life may convey to us a unique illumination of the whole mystery of our existence, because in these actions and realities . . . something "numinous" is resident, something holy and gracious.[15]

The bread and the wine that are used in the Eucharist are the most basic elements of ordinary life. Yet through them the sacred is revealed. Scott says, "For bread and wine could not be set apart for consecration unless ours were in some basic sense a sacramental universe and unless rivers and trees and tractors and spinning wheels were also eligible to be considered as 'sacramentals.'"[16] We live in what Scott calls "a sacramental universe" because it is through the elements of the ordinary world that the sacred is revealed.

Pierre Teilhard de Chardin offers us a further example of this "sacramental" thinking based on the Incarnation. In his poetic essay, "The Mass on the World," Teilhard, a Catholic priest, finds himself far from the established, formal setting for the mass, yet wishes to offer the sacrifice and so celebrate his "mass on the world."

> Since once again, Lord—though this time not in the forests of the Aisne but in the steppes of Asia—I have neither bread, nor wine, nor altar, I will raise myself beyond these symbols, up to the pure majesty of the real itself; I, your priest, will make the whole earth my altar and on it will offer you all the labours and sufferings of the world.[17]

As he goes on in his celebration of the mass, he makes this crucial statement: "Through your own incarnation, my God, all matter is henceforth incarnate."[18] The sacrament is possible because of the act of the Incarnation of God in Jesus Christ. And because of this, human existence within this world is affirmed as the way and place of revelation of the sacred. One need not flee the world to find God. The life, death, and resurrection of Jesus Christ reveal that it

[15]Nathan A. Scott, Jr., *The Wild Prayer of Longing: Poetry and the Sacred* (New Haven: Yale University Press, 1971), p. 49.

[16]Ibid., p. 51.

[17]Pierre Teilhard de Chardin, *Hymn of the Universe*, trans. Simon Bartholomew (New York: Harper & Row, 1965), p. 19.

[18]Ibid., p. 24.

is through the world that the transformation takes place, that salvation occurs.

The Incarnation and Literature

William F. Lynch, S. J., presents an understanding of the creative imagination and its relationship, analogically, to Christology that illumines the idea of the Incarnation as a model for literature. Lynch begins with the existential situation of all human beings: finitude and limitation. In being limited, we are also particular.

> The human imagination responds in various ways to the vision that is borne in upon it of universal limitation, or particularity. . . . No matter what form the vision takes, however, or what its final goal—whether that be beauty, or insight, or peace, or tranquillity, or God—the heart, substance, and center of the human imagination, as of human life, must lie in the particular and limited image or thing.
>
> In this world there are generalities about things, but there are no generalities. If people and things were themselves generalities, they would be far more tractable than they are. [19]

His view is that the imagination's power lies in its analogical function. His thought parallels Paul Ricoeur's as he asserts that in analogy one cannot make a simple, external distinction between the image and its object. In some comparisons we are able to stand outside of the image and to differentiate exactly between how the image is like an object and how it is different. In analogy as Lynch uses the term, however, this is not possible. There is an interpenetration between the sameness and the difference, and between the literal and secondary content, that makes it impossible to separate the two. If it were possible to separate them, one could discard the literal meaning after seeing the secondary meaning; one could throw away the symbol after seeing what it pointed to. But the power of analogy lies precisely in the fact that this cannot be done. One must participate fully in the action of the details if one is to experience the wholeness of the pattern.

> There are people who are afraid that the pattern, the taste, the atmosphere, will suffer from the emergence of the detail. But how can it if detail is the life of the pattern and is the pattern itself, and if every detail can in its own way sing with the whole of the pattern? There are those, reversely, who are afraid the detail, the freedom, the exalted unpredictability of the world and of the imagination, will suffer from the pattern. [20]

---

[19] William F. Lynch, S. J., *Christ and Apollo: The Dimensions of the Literary Imagination*, (New York: New American Library, 1963), pp. 20–21.
[20] Ibid., p. 148.

We are reminded of Yeats's image of the dancer and the dance. Only in the movement of the details and the pattern together can either be revealed. Thus, the artist must work with the particularities of images of limitation:

> [They] are in themselves the path to whatever the self is seeking: to insight, or beauty, or, for that matter, to God. This path is both narrow and direct; it leads, I believe, straight through our human realities, through our labor, our disappointments, our friends, our game legs, our harvests, our subjection to time. There are no shortcuts to beauty or to insight. We must go *through* the finite, the limited, the definite, omitting none of it lest we omit some of the potencies of being-in-the-flesh.[21]

We are here at the heart of Lynch's aesthetic. He began with the undeniable fact that we are of the world. We are finite and limited. To deal with reality, then, it is necessary to deal with the things of the world, with what is limited and finite. However, there is more at work here than resigned realism. Lynch firmly believes that the order of the world is such that by going through the world, through the exploration of finitude, something more than the finite is achieved—insight or beauty on a secular level, God on the religious level. The reason for his faith in the finite to lead causally and creatively toward insight lies in his Christology.

> It is no small wonder that it is in Christ we come to the fullest possible understanding of what analogy means in the fullest concrete, the facing relentlessly into the two poles of the same and the different and the interpenetrating reconciliation of the two contraries. . . . It is the universal teaching of the Church that it was itself born . . . out of His blood, at a set hour, in a set place.
>
> In that place and hour was brought about the wedding of the altogether unique and different Thing (down to the last drop of blood) and the ultimate society of the Church (the same). These two things, by virtue of a very great mystery, cannot be separated from each other. And this, their common mystery of identity, stands as the model for every analogical act of the imagination.[22]

As the conflict between sameness and difference is resolved in the model of Christ, so is the conflict between the concrete and the unlimited, the particular (details) and the universal (pattern):

> The attitude I am proposing as a model . . . is exemplified in Christology, where the conflict has been resolved once and for all, I believe, in a continuous, open, and dynamic way. . . . We would be disparaging Christ and disparaging the finite if we were to assign to Him an improperly transcendent character and were to assign to the finite, through which He walked, any negative or deprecatory quality.

[21]Ibid., p. 23.
[22]Ibid., p. 158.

He is stressing the Incarnation, the embodiment of the divine in human form. His view of Christ is that it is through his embodiment into the particularities of limitation that he draws all persons to himself. It is not *in spite* of his humanity, but *because* of it that the transformative power of God is revealed.

> With every plunge through, or down into, the real contours of being, the imagination also shoots up into insight, but in such a way that the plunge down *causally generates* the plunge up. This movement might be diagrammed as:[23]

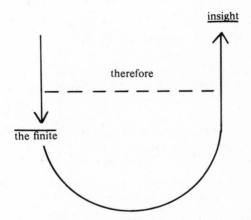

By the passage through the finite something comes into being that would otherwise have remained unrealized.

We have gone into detail about Lynch's theory of the imagination and his Christology because he presents a good example of how a literary critic can utilize a Christian doctrine to formulate an aesthetic. As you might suppose, in his discussion of literary works, he is quite critical of those who seem to affirm something at the cost of denial of the world or who search out the finite and find nothing there or beyond it to affirm. Such an investigation can be very useful, but one must keep in mind the danger of rejecting as useless or false a portrayal of reality that does not immediately fit Lynch's pattern. One must search to discover what the artist is revealing and if one comes to a work with a predetermined view of what *should* be revealed there is little chance that the work of art will be experienced for what it is in itself. And there is no chance that one's religious understanding will be extended beyond the limits with which one approaches the work.

On the side of literature, on the other hand, we must recognize the danger of creating a work that runs counter to Lynch's analysis. Allen Tate uses the term "angelic imagination" to refer to literature that disavows the world in its incarnate concreteness. He quotes from Jacques Maritain's *The Dream of Descartes:*

> Cartesian dualism breaks man up into two complete substances, joined to one another none knows how: on the one hand, the body which is only geometrical extension; on the other, the soul which is only thought—an angel inhabiting a machine and directing it by means of the pineal gland.[24]

The imagination that results from this view of the world seeks to operate as independently as possible from the givenness of creation. It refuses to "hold on hard to the huckleberry bushes," believing that the imagination's function is to escape the bounds of the earth. To the contrary, Tate and Maritain assert the imagination must begin with the materials of the world. Imagination relies on sense perception; it begins with what is concretely perceivable. As Joyce Cary points out, you look at a picture by feeling it with your eye. We could say you read a novel by feeling it with your eyes and your ears. What is finally revealed through these sensuous details is "the jug of jugs and the woman of women." But that jug and woman are reached only through the very real, concrete details of the world we live in. The angelic imagination would wish to short circuit this process and leap immediately to the jug of jugs, without bothering with the particular jug that has full weight and shape and color. But that is not how the imagination or the creations of the imagination work. The symbols by which a novel or a poem or a painting can speak to us have their beginning point, their roots, in the earth. Using Lynch's term, analogy, we would say that the analogy must be *to* something. And that something is the world we know.

The principle of incarnation is of great importance for literature. The imagination must work with the materials of this world. The Christian doctrine of Incarnation parallels this process but gives the added affirmation that by way of the passage through this world there is a "more" that is achieved.

The Affirmation of Roethke

We see this process at work in the poetry of Theodore Roethke. Although Roethke is not a "Christian" poet, he is

[24]Allen Tate, "The Angelic Imagination," *The Man of Letters in the Modern World* (Cleveland: World Publishing Co., 1955), p. 122.

ultimately concerned with the life of the spirit. For him the life of the spirit is nurtured and grows through the concrete particulars of this world. Much of Roethke's poetry involves the things of the natural world—plants, birds, creatures. Through the relationship he has with them, we see the growth of his own spirit *within* the incarnate, physical world. In the poem "Moss-Gathering" we see the care the speaker has for the things of the world and we see how this affirmation of particular living things grows out of an understanding of the wholeness of existence that transcends all particular things. He begins by describing in intricate detail the appearance of the moss:

> To loosen with all ten fingers held wide and limber
> And lift up a patch, dark-green, the kind for lining cemetery baskets,
> Thick and cushiony, like an old-fashioned doormat,
> The crumbling small hollow sticks on the underside mixed with roots,
> And wintergreen berries and leaves still stuck to the top,—
> That was moss-gathering.

Having created for us the particularity of the moss and the act of gathering it, he goes on to describe what he learns about the significance of this act:

> But something always went out of me when I dug loose those carpets
> Of green, or plunged to my elbows in the spongy yellowish moss of the
>   marshes:
> And afterwards I always felt mean, jogging back over the logging road,
> As if I had broken the natural order of things in that swampland;
> Disturbed some rhythm, old and of vast importance,
> By pulling off flesh from the living planet;
> As if I had committed, against the whole scheme of life, a desecration.[25]

The whole earth is seen as a living organism, incarnate and inspirited. A human being is part of this community of living things because men and women, too, are embodied and inspirited. Thus the poet feels a sense of connectedness to, and responsibility for, the concrete world around him. Roethke is using the technique of personification here, attributing to nonhuman things human characteristics. This is a form of analogy. But analogy here, as in our discussion of Lynch, is more than a formal technique of bringing two unlike things together. In Roethke's poem we feel that the livingness of the planet and the "scheme of life" that his moss-gathering disturbs, are, in fact, reality. We are applying human terms to the nonhuman because these are the only words

---

[25] *The Collected Poems of Theodore Roethke* (Garden City, N. Y.: Doubleday & Co., 1966), p. 40. The following quotations are taken from this edition.

we can use to describe what is felt to be an *actual* relationship between the human and the nonhuman. The poet *is* a part of the scheme that includes and transcends the whole universe. Through his care for moss—such a simple, common thing that we, without a second thought, walk on, pull up, disregard—he asks us to take another look, really to see the concrete particulars of the world. In doing so he, and we, if the poem works, discover through one insignificant, unique thing the wholeness that gives meaning to all things.

In "A Light Breather" he speaks directly of the human spirit. But how does he go about trying to understand and give expression to this ephemeral reality of human experience?—through the things we know in the physical world. As is customary with Roethke, it is through the nonhuman things that we come to understand the most precious human things.

> The spirit moves,
> yet stays:
> Stirs as a blossom stirs,
> Still wet from its bud-sheath,
> Slowly unfolding,
> Turning in the light with its tendrils;
> Plays as a minnow plays,
> Tethered to a limp weed, swinging,
> Tail around, nosing in and out of the current,
> Its shadows loose, a watery finger;
> Moves, like the snail,
> Still inward,
> Taking and embracing its surroundings,
> Never wishing itself away,
> Unafraid of what it is,
> A music in a hood,
> A small thing,
> Singing.
>
> (P. 101)

Roethke is using analogy to describe the life of the spirit: it stirs as a blossom stirs; plays as a minnow plays; moves like the snail, still inward. Through these three images from the natural world, the life of the spirit unfolds before us. The blossoming of the bud, the minnow moving with its environment, the snail, moving inward yet not denying its surroundings, affirming both itself and its world—all these reveal in a simple image the life of the spirit. The poem gives us this image not by fleeing from the physical but by going *through* the physical. We should also note that while these images from the natural world are used to try to reach the human spirit, the things of the world themselves are also important. We see the poet's care for the blossom, the minnow, the snail—as well as for the spirit. It is only through these that one reaches the spirit. We cannot say the spirit is like a minnow in this way and then disregard the minnow. The spirit is *like* the snail, but only by staying with the image of the "music in a hood" can we experience the reality of the spirit. It is known only through embodiment.

In a final example, "The Manifestation," Roethke explicitly uses the term analogy and shows us again how only through the realities of this world can we come to know the transcendent that gives meaning to the world.

> Many arrivals make us live: the tree becoming
> Green, a bird tipping the topmost bough,
> A seed pushing itself beyond itself,
> The mole making its way through darkest ground,
> The worm, intrepid scholar of the soil—
> Do these analogies perplex? A sky with clouds,
> The motion of the moon, and waves at play,
> A sea-wind pausing in a summer tree.
>
> What does what it should do needs nothing more.
> The body moves, though slowly, toward desire.
> We come to something without knowing why.

(P. 235)

The poem begins, "Many arrivals make us live," and the rest of the stanza is the unfolding of the meaning of that statement. Five images are given that describe growing things either as they begin or as they are renewed or in their steady progression through the earth. We sense life in these images, and in sensing it we are called back to life ourselves. These images are not only of things that are obviously life-giving: the bird and the sprouting seed—but also of the mole and the worm: the underside of life. All living things are a manifestation of life. But there is another dimension as well. These images not only describe how we gain new life from observing and participating in it through these other forms of life, they also are analogies for the forms of life, the new arrivals, that are within ourselves. We learn to live through the bird—the skipping, graceful spirit—and also through the mole—that underground, preconscious world within us.

The poet then asks, "Do these analogies perplex?" and goes on to give four more images, this time of nature itself. Each of these presents a careful conjunction of being and becoming, of enduring and changing, of stillness and motion. As the world of nature is sustained through the commingling of these contradictory elements, so are we.

The second stanza tells us that the fulfillment of who we are is all we can hope for or wish. As we discover that we are living creatures who have within us the power of love and sympathy and the power of spirit, then we can move toward desire—toward, not away from, the world we live in and the people and creatures of that world. It is here, in this world, among the things of nature, that the manifestation occurs and wholeness and peace are found.

The Questioning of Sartre

Roethke takes the principle of incarnation seriously, and by his immersion in and acceptance of the reality of the created world, the life of the spirit grows. The world of Roquentin, the main character in Jean-Paul Sartre's *Nausea,* is quite another case. We will look briefly at this novel. It is written in the form of the diary of Antoine Roquentin. He begins this diary because of a strange occurrence he hopes to try to understand. What he discovers is also a discovery for us as readers. The initial experience that troubles Roquentin involves a stone he picked up at the seashore. He describes the stone in this way: "The stone was flat and dry, especially on one side, damp and muddy on the other. I held it by the edges with my fingers wide apart so as not to get them dirty."[26] What he can't explain is the great disgust he experiences—so much disgust that he feels compelled to drop the stone and flee from it. He later describes this disgust as nausea.

Roquentin recognizes his isolation from other human beings from the beginning. What he discovers, which is related to this human isolation, is the isolation of all things. Nothing is related; everything is contingent. This fact is forced on him by the objects of the world. Once again we have an emphasis on the concreteness of things, but his response to this discovery is quite the opposite of Roethke's. After a number of "nauseating" experiences, he begins to understand his relation to the stone that was the occasion for beginning his diary. "I was going to throw that pebble, I looked at it and then it all began: I felt that it *existed"* (p. 165). Why should this cause him so much distress? Things in their existence are beyond the categories that human beings try to impose on them in order to control them. We use words to capture a thing; we talk about its function to make it amenable to our view of an orderly world. But when it comes down to it, Roquentin discovers, things

---

[26]Jean-Paul Sartre, *Nausea,* trans. Lloyd Alexander (New York: New Directions Publishing Corp., 1964), p. 8. The following quotations are taken from this edition.

(including human beings) *simply exist*. We try to force them into meaningful arrangements by seeing the relationships between them, but this is merely human illusion. Existence is unquestionable and is absurd.

Roquentin's central vision of this reality occurs when he encounters a chestnut tree, experiences it in its stark existence, and is filled with and understands Nausea.

> So I was in the park just now. The roots of the chestnut tree were sunk in the ground just under my bench. I couldn't remember it was a root any more. The words had vanished and with them the significance of things, their methods of use, and the feeble points of reference which men have traced on their surface. I was sitting, stooping forward, head bowed, alone in front of this black, knotty mass, entirely beastly, which frightened me. Then I had this vision.
>
> It left me breathless. Never, until these last few days, had I understood the meaning of "existence." . . . And then all of a sudden, there it was, clear as day: existence had suddenly unveiled itself. It had lost the harmless look of an abstract category: it was the very paste of things, this root was kneaded into existence. . . . [The] veneer had melted, leaving soft, monstrous masses, all in disorder—naked, in a frightful, obscene nakedness. . . . All these objects . . . how can I explain? They inconvenienced me; I would have liked them to exist less strongly, more dryly, in a more abstract way, with more reserve. The chestnut tree **pressed** itself against my eyes. (Pp. 170–72)

Having felt things in their impenetrable reality, he senses the utter meaninglessness of their being at all. He sees this as *absolutely* absurd because it is absurdity in relation to nothing else, since no real relationships exist. The root of the chestnut tree is absurd, but there is nothing in relation to which it is absurd—which leaves us nothing to hold on to, nothing that is not absurd. His response to this revelation is Nausea.

> I understood the Nausea, I possessed it. . . . The essential thing is contingency. I mean that one cannot define existence as necessity. To exist is simply *to be there*; . . . all these existents which bustled about this tree came from nowhere and were going nowhere. Suddenly they existed, then suddenly they existed no longer: existence is without memory; of the vanished it retains nothing—not even a memory. Existence everywhere, infinitely, in excess, for ever and everywhere; existence—which is limited only by existence. . . . Every existing thing is born without reason, prolongs itself out of weakness and dies by chance. . . . Existence is a fullness which man can never abandon. (Pp. 176–80)

The embodiment we discussed in relation to Roethke's poetry is certainly present here. But what a contrast between the joy at creation found in Roethke's poetry and the nausea that is experienced here! Sartre even uses some of the terms that might be found in Roethke's poetry, but in this context they become repulsive to us:

> I sank down on the bench, stupefied, stunned by this profusion of beings without origin: everywhere blossomings, hatchings out, my ears buzzed with existence, my very flesh throbbed and opened, abandoned itself to the universal burgeoning. It was repugnant. But why, I thought, why so many existences, since they all look alike? . . . So many existences missed, obstinately begun again and again missed—like the awkward efforts of an insect fallen on its back? (I was one of those efforts.) That abundance did not give the effect of generosity, just the opposite. (Pp. 178–79)

Martin Heidegger describes the astonishment and joy that human beings can feel as they experience the reality of existence and cry, "Why is there something rather than nothing?" Roquentin's response to the reality of existence is to say,

> The naked World suddenly reveal[ed] itself, and I choked with rage at this gross, absurd being. You couldn't even wonder where all that sprang from, or how it was that a world came into existence, rather than nothingness. (Pp. 180–81)

If one could wonder, presumably, it would be with anger and resentment rather than astonishment and joy. What is it that brings Roquentin to this experience of existence? A study of the existentialist philosophy of Sartre would be necessary to explore this question thoroughly. But we can say briefly that existentialism is a modern philosophy that grows out of the breakdown of the certainties that provided a secure structure out of which human beings could operate. Necessary to this structure was the belief in a God who had created the world and human beings and who ordered existence meaningfully. Without this belief, orderliness and meaningful relations seem to disappear. Nothing makes a difference if there is no pattern, no plan to existence. The existentialist response has been to say that human beings must create their own meaning, since none is *given* to them, in the face of a universe that is essentially absurd.

In *Nausea* we see hints of a possible meaning Roquentin could create in the few moments of happiness he has while he is listening to music. Music does not *exist,* he says, because it has a meaningful order. It has a beginning and an end, and the end directs and puts into significant relations all that comes before it. This could be a description of human existence seen from the Judeo-Christian point of view. But for Roquentin that view is lost. Only that which does not really exist—art is the possibility that is offered in this novel—can have any meaning at all. Roquentin at the end of the novel is contemplating writing a novel which would parallel the music and have significance outside of existence. To do this he must struggle to overcome existence, overcome the thingness of things, which is utterly destructive. This is quite the opposite of Roethke's entry *into* the world of things as a way of discovering meaning. And it is finally the rejection of the principle of incarnation.

We must take the way of Jean-Paul Sartre seriously. The novel he has written reflects much of the lived experience of the twentieth century. We cannot dismiss it because it does not satisfy our affirmation, both for religion and for literature, of the embodied, concrete world (although of course in his writing Sartre uses concrete details very effectively to make us experience the Nausea). Sartre reveals very clearly incarnation without transcendence. This is the experience of despair that is real to many people in the contemporary world: that there is nothing to be gained by going through the concrete; that it is only by escaping it that life can be affirmed. This view of the world would provide us with a different aesthetic and a different theology than we have been discussing under the rubric "incarnation." But to take seriously Sartre's novel and to seek out the aesthetic and theology that would coincide with Roquentin's vision would be to open new possibilities for understanding the contemporary world and our own experiences of it.

THE FALL

A second theme that often becomes the subject of discussion in literature is the Christian doctrine of the Fall or Original Sin. The terms refer to the story of the temptation and fall from grace of Adam and Eve. Very early in the Christian tradition the myth of Adam and the myth of Christ were closely associated. In the book of Romans in the New Testament, Paul establishes a relationship between the "first Adam" and the "second Adam" (Christ):

> As one man's trespass led to condemnation for all men, so one man's act of righteousness leads to acquittal and life for all men. For as by one man's disobedience many were made sinners, so by one man's obedience many will be made righteous. (Romans 5:18–19)

In the Christian tradition, the myth of the Fall is understood in relation to the saving action of Christ.

Within the context of this relationship, what is the meaning of the Fall? First, the story in Genesis is a way of understanding evil in the world. We know from the opening chapter of Genesis that the world and human beings are created good. How then does evil enter in? Through a free choice by Adam, with the help of the serpent and Eve. What is it about this free choice that is sinful? God has told Adam not to eat of the tree of the knowledge of good and evil. The serpent says, "Your eyes will be opened, and you will be like God, knowing good and evil" (Gen. 3:5). To disobey God and to try to be like God is Adam's sin. Reinhold Niebuhr explains human sin in this way:

> Man is insecure and involved in natural contingency; he seeks to overcome his insecurity by a will-to-power which overreaches the limits of human creatureliness. Man is ignorant and involved in the limitations of a finite mind; but he pretends that he is not limited. He assumes that he can gradually transcend finite limitations until his mind becomes identical with universal mind. All of his intellectual and cultural pursuits, therefore, become infected with the sin of pride. Man's pride and will-to-power disturb the harmony of creation.[27]

There is a deviation from what is intended in God's plan for creation.[28] It is a deviation by overreaching. The letter of Paul to the Philippians presents another comparison between the first and second Adam. Adam wished to be like God. Paul says to the Church at Philippi:

> Have this mind among yourselves, which you have in Christ Jesus, who, though he was in the form of God, did not count equality with God a thing to be grasped, but emptied himself, taking the form of a servant, being born in the likeness of men. And being found in human form he humbled himself and became obedient unto death, even death on a cross. (Philippians 2:5-8)

The sin of Adam, a human being, was to try to be like God. The righteousness of Christ, the Son of God, was humbly to take on human form.

The consequences of Adam's sin, as we saw in the first quotation from Romans, is that all people are in sin. Whether we take this to be a genetic fault that is passed from generation to generation or whether we see each person as, with free will, repeating the sin of Adam, the message in Christianity is clear. While having free will, human beings sin. The possibility of redemption from this sin comes through the life, death, and resurrection of Jesus Christ. Human beings do not share the

[27]Reinhold Niebuhr, *The Nature and Destiny of Man: A Christian Interpretation*, vol. 1: *Human Nature*, 1 vol. ed. (New York: Charles Scribner's Sons, 1953), pp. 178–79.

[28]Ricoeur, *Symbolism of Evil*, p. 233.

innocence of Adam before the Fall. But they do share the promise of redemption through Christ.

Literary Uses of the Doctrine of the Fall

When we look at works of literature we see many examples of human beings overreaching themselves and ending in destruction. We see characters who are clearly living with the consequences of sin, experiencing alienation and guilt. We see the impact of finitude and lack of perfection as characters discover they are not innocent and are apt to cause more destruction by thinking they are. Are we then to say that all such works of literature are "Christian" and are operating in terms of the doctrine of Original Sin?

Although it can be very useful in examining religious dimensions of literature to discuss the Christian doctrine of Original Sin and the Fall, there are dangers that one must be aware of. There is first the danger of coming to a work of literature with this doctrine in mind and "explaining" the work in terms of it. This would prevent us from really seeing what was present in the work. We would have imposed our category on the art work without giving it a chance to speak to us. A second danger lies in asserting that we are talking about the Christian doctrine of Original Sin but meaning by that simply human finitude. R. W. B. Lewis and Sallie TeSelle (McFague) both warn against making all writers "Christian" who reveal the fallibility and suffering of human beings. In fact, such a writer may be very far from Christian doctrine if there is not also present in the work of art the message of redemption. R. W. B. Lewis says,

> Separated from the rich theological framework within which it historically evolved, the concept of Original Sin is not much of a concept at all; it is more an image of unredeemably depraved human nature shivering somewhere in the void.[29]

Sallie TeSelle (McFague) quotes another critic, Randall Stewart, commenting on the presence of the concept of Original Sin in Faulkner:

> Faulkner embodies and dramatizes the basic Christian concepts so effectively that he can with justice be regarded as one of the most profoundly Christian writers in our time. There is everywhere in his writings the basic premise of Original Sin; everywhere the conflict between the flesh and the spirit. . . . Man in Faulkner is a heroic, tragic figure.[30]

[29]Lewis, "Hold on Hard," p. 99.
[30]Randall Stewart, *American Literature and Christian Doctrine,* cited by TeSelle

TeSelle (McFague) asserts that this emphasis, both in Stewart and in Faulkner, is "preincarnational." Original Sin as a tragic dimension of existence is present only when there is not the promise of the life, death, and resurrection of Jesus Christ. Human life after the Fall is no longer tragic in light of the resurrection.

If we look at the other side of this question of the Christian view of the nature of human beings, we will notice that one must also be careful when attributing the title of Christian to writers who portray the innocence and goodness of their characters. Although Adam before the Fall is called "innocent" and although goodness is seen within the Christian tradition as an ideal to be strived for, human beings live "after the fall." Their goodness is always limited and, in the Christian view, always dependent on the grace of God. Although an innocent character may be said to be "Christ-like," human beings are never Christ but are always caught in the ambiguity of a life lived between goodness and evil.

If we are aware of these dangers of imposing a doctrine on literature and of seeing a doctrine in literature that is there only in partial form, how, then, can we talk about Original Sin and the Fall in exploring religious dimensions of literature? We can begin with literature itself. If, as we have said above, human beings are always caught in the ambiguity between goodness and evil, then, in order to create realistic characters who have the power to convince us in their struggles, their joys, their despair, the artist must present characters who share in this human situation. T. S. Eliot, using the category of Original Sin as an assumption for his criticism, makes this comment:

> With the disappearance of the idea of Original Sin, with the disappearance of the idea of intense moral struggle, the human beings presented to us both in poetry and in prose fiction today and more patently among the serious writers than in the underworld of letters, tend to become less and less real. It is in fact in moments of moral and spiritual struggle depending upon spiritual sanctions, rather than in those "bewildering minutes" in which we are all very much alike, that men and women come nearest to being real.[31]

Although we must be cautious of Eliot's assumption that the idea of Original Sin has disappeared or that it could not present itself in modern literature in unexpected forms, his point about the "reality" of both actual people and characters in a work of literature is well taken. Sallie TeSelle (McFague) says, "Very simply, this belief about man results in better art—in a poem or novel that

(McFague), *Literature*, p. 23.

[31]T. S. Eliot, *After Strange Gods: A Primer of Modern Heresy*, cited by TeSelle (McFague), *Literature*, pp. 24–25.

is complex, ironical, and paradoxical, reflecting the reality of man as both good and evil."[32] Thus, it would be useful to talk about the Christian doctrine of the Fall in relation to a novel written by a person who might have no knowledge of the concept or intention of using it. The concept of the Fall might well illumine, in Christian terms, the reality of the human situation revealed by the characters.

Such a procedure does not turn artists into Christians. It does not require that they use the terminology of Christian doctrine or present it in an orthodox manner. In addition, it leaves the work of literature free to reveal something new to us or to reveal something old in an unexpected way. If we discover through a careful reading of a novel that themes such as guilt, disobedience, and power (overreaching and deviation in our earlier terms) are important, then it may well be helpful in understanding the novel to talk about them in terms of the mythic structures of Original Sin and the Fall. Our awareness of the meaning of these doctrines may also be increased by the creation within the novel of these human problems in a new way. In order for literature to reveal something to us of the religious situation of human beings in terms of the Fall, it is not necessary that the writer present the Christian message. Although we would not call the writer Christian, it may be that, in Tillich's terms, the literature can present the question to which the Christian doctrine can provide the answer.[33] That is, a novel may reveal the fallen condition of human beings without any way of overcoming this condition. But through the compelling presentation of the problem, we may be made more aware of the situation of despair in which we find ourselves before the presence of the sacred is revealed.

Nathan Scott points out in his essay, "Poetry and Prayer," that much of the literature of the modern period presents a very negative picture of the human condition, a view quite in contrast to the Christian vision. He sees the writers of our period as "forging an image of the human creature as one ousted from the precincts of security and grace."[34] He uses the terms "impoverishment and indigence" to describe the condition of human beings in our time. But he goes on to say, what can we ask of our writers? If we live in a time whose spirit is secular, a time when alienation and despair

---

[32]TeSelle (McFague), *Literature,* p. 22.

[33]Paul Tillich, *Theology of Culture,* ed. Robert C. Kimball (New York: Oxford University Press, 1964), p. 49.

[34]Nathan A. Scott, Jr., *Negative Capability: Studies in the New Literature and the Religious Situation* (New Haven: Yale University Press, 1969), p. 106.

dominate and the accesses to the sacred are largely unknown, then our writers must present this reality if they are to speak to our situation.

> We have, all of us, so to speak, "fallen" into the Profane, and the historian of religion Mircea Eliade suggests that "desacralization" is the category that most comprehensively describes the spiritual situation of modern man. So our literature, if it is to be an authentically contemporary literature, will inevitably be secular, and the world which it describes will be a world in which God appears in some way to have disappeared.[35]

But if it is the case that modern literature cannot, because of its commitment to the reality of the age in which we live, present the full image of the human condition as it is envisioned in the New Testament—human beings as living after the Fall, but also after the resurrection—then does this literature offer nothing in our search for manifestations of religion in literature? To the contrary, Scott believes that there is, from the Christian standpoint, much to be gained through the experience of this "secular" literature.

> And not only will ours be a secular literature, but I would myself hope that it would be radically secular, since skepticism and negation and denial may, if they are profound enough, by reason of their very radicalism, begin to quicken sensibilities of another order that are now either being put aside or declining into atrophy. In the degree to which it deepens the sense of religious deprivation, a radically secular literature may, in other words, by a dialectical route bring us once again into proximity to the Presence that we had thought to be absent—and thus it may become itself a kind of witness to the Indestructible.[36]

We may, then, discover something of the actuality of our fallen situation through the most secular literature and, through it, be brought to a recovery of the sacred.

After the Fall

Arthur Miller's play *After the Fall* will serve as an example of a work that uses the religious symbolism of the Fall. The play has as some of its central concerns the German concentration camps and the extermination of the Jews, the McCarthy anti-communist hearings in the 1950s, and the difficulties the main character, Quentin, has with these issues. The question of guilt and innocence dominates the play; and, as the title indicates, the truth that is revealed is that we are not innocent but live "after the fall." The

---

[35]Ibid., p. 109.
[36]Ibid., pp. 109–10.

fall then becomes the symbol for the guilt that we, as members of the human community, are party to and must take responsibility for. We wish to be innocent and not to hurt other people, but this can occur only if we refuse to become involved with other people. In our involvement we must take responsibility for our own sins and those of our community. The image of Adam sinning and all other people sinning because of this is indirectly expressed here. Because we are all "related" we are guilty of crimes we may not personally have committed. For example, the death camps are our responsibility as much as that of any Germans who worked in them. "No one they didn't kill can be innocent again,"[37] Holga, a woman he meets in Germany, tells him. We cannot be innocent because we share the responsibility for the actions of all human beings. And we do so because we are like them. We are guilty because we are filled with joy that it was not we who died in the concentration camps.

One of Quentin's friends is being investigated by the House Un-American Activities Committee, and Quentin agrees to be his lawyer and vows to stick by him to the end. But for all his words and actions of support, when his friend commits suicide by falling in front of a commuter train, Quentin is filled with joy, because the danger to himself, brought on by defending an accused communist, is now gone. He fears this is a characteristic of all people:

> Good fathers, devoted sons, grateful that someone else will die, not they, and how can one understand that, if one is innocent? If somewhere in one's soul there is no accomplice—of that joy, that joy, that joy when a burden dies . . . and leaves you safe? (P. 83)

This is one of the important discoveries Quentin makes. We want to believe we are innocent; we act as if we were innocent. But we are not. And pretending that we are, denying our guilt, only causes more destruction. Quentin says at one point, still unable to accept his guilt, his fallenness:

> It's that if there is love, it must be limitless; a love not even of persons but blind, blind to insult, blind to the spear in the flesh, like justice blind, like . . . (P. 143)

But, in fact, love is not like that—not human love after the fall. By asserting that that is what love must be—and often attributing such love to oneself—one is prevented from really loving, from admitting one's shortcomings, selfishness, and unfaithfulness—one's guilt—and from loving in the imperfect way that is the only way human beings are capable of loving. As the marriage with his

---

[37]Arthur Miller, *After the Fall* (New York: Bantam Books, 1965), p. 30. The following quotations are taken from this edition.

second wife is dissolving and she is attempting suicide with barbituates, he says that they loved the innocence in each other. They refused to admit their guilt. They tried to destroy the guilt in each other so only the innocence would remain. But in so doing, they could only destroy each other, because no one is innocent.

Holga, who seems to possess the wisdom through suffering that Quentin is seeking, talks about her struggles.

> The same dream returned each night until I dared not go to sleep and grew quite ill. I dreamed I had a child, and even in the dream I saw it was my life, and it was an idiot, and I ran away. But it always crept onto my lap again, clutched at my clothes. Until I thought, if I could kiss it, whatever in it was my own, perhaps I could sleep. And I bent to its broken face, and it was horrible . . . but I kissed it. I think one must finally take one's life in one's arms. (Pp. 30–31)

What Quentin is unable to understand is how a person who has faced this idiot, one's guilty life, can continue to hope as Holga does. He says at the first of the play as he begins to recount his story, that every morning he wakes up as a boy, filled with hope. Using the language of the symbol of the Fall, we would say that he wakes up as Adam before the Fall. "For an instant there's some—unformed promise in the air. . . . And then, it seeps in my room, my life and its pointlessness. And I thought—if I could corner that hope, find what it consists of and either kill it for a lie, or really make it mine" (p. 5). At the conclusion of his story, and the end of the play, he begins to understand both Holga's hope and his own.

> That woman hopes! . . . Or is that . . . exactly why she hopes, because she knows? What burning cities taught her and the death of love taught me: that we are very dangerous! . . . And that, that's why I wake each morning like a boy—even now, even now! I swear to you, I could love the world again! Is the knowing all? To know, and even happily, that we meet unblessed; not in some garden of wax fruit and painted trees, that lie of Eden, but after, after the Fall, after many, many deaths. Is the knowing all? And the wish to kill is never killed, but with some gift of courage one may look into its face when it appears, and with a stroke of love—as to an idiot in the house—forgive it; again and again . . . forever? (Pp. 162–63)

Miller presents with great intensity the conflict of the longing for innocence and the reality of guilt in human life. He uses primarily social images that are a part of our consciousness as people living in the twentieth century to reveal this situation. For people in the contemporary world, the Nazi death camps become the symbol of the reality of the Fall. However, we might want to say, although the significance of this event is unquestionable, there are other events; there is the event in the garden for example. The Fall is not something that occurred in 1940, but rather with the beginning of the human race. Miller uses this modern event to give cogency to a myth that may have lost its significance for many living in this time. Of course, the use of the religious symbolism that goes back to the garden of Eden enriches this modern dramatization of our guilt. It turns it from a sociological or political event into a mythic event in which we all participate. It becomes a modern symbol for the reality of human sinfulness in all aspects of life.

The image of the Fall is presented with great power. But what about the image of redemption that is the counterpart to the Adamic myth? The answer that Miller's characters come to in the face of human guilt involves "knowledge," "some gift of courage," and "a stroke of love." The last two items may certainly have something in common with the gift of grace, although the traditional symbols of grace are not present as is the traditional symbol of guilt, the Fall. It may be that this contemporary writer, while being able to delineate fully the despair of the Fall, can only point in the direction of the answer that is revealed through Jewish and Christian symbols. Nonetheless, *After the Fall* is of great significance for understanding religious dimensions of our culture as it creates for us in stark and moving terms the meaning of the Fall in contemporary images and as it points—necessarily ambiguously in our time—to a grace that abounds after the Fall.

HISTORICAL AND CYCLICAL TIME

The final theme we will examine is time. We will look at the religious understanding of this element of life and the role it plays in literature. It is related to the previous themes in Christian doctrine, the Incarnation and the Fall, because they both presuppose and affirm the importance of historical existence. In addition, the historical dimension is crucial to Jewish religious understanding.

Time is a very complex element in ordering and understanding our world. Although we are all very much aware of its presence, if we were asked to explain to someone what time was, we might have a great deal of difficulty. In *The Confessions* Augustine said, "What is time? When you do not ask me, I know; but when you ask me, I no longer know" (bk. 11). We will discuss here three aspects of the experience of time relevant for an inquiry into religious dimensions of literature.

One experience of time is the historical. This can be called linear time because it moves in a line from one new moment to the next. We have the experience of linear time as we see ourselves growing and changing and moving finally toward death. We see this in animals and plants in the natural world. We also see it in a much broader framework in the evolution of the earth, both organically and inorganically. But within this realm of change we also experience a second element, which we can call duration. If all were completely new at each moment there would be no continuity, no connection between the past, present, and future. And our experience of the world is that this continuity exists. Thus, within historical time we experience both change and duration.

There is a third experience of time we observe when we examine both the natural world and our ways of measuring time. The hands of a clock move around in a circle. A year has 365 days and then we begin with the first day once again. The seasons recur once each year. We see in the natural world that a flower grows, blossoms, turns to seed, and dies. But the next spring the process is repeated. Thus, our experience of time is cyclical as well as linear.

Religious understandings of time involve all three elements. Cyclical myths are common to archaic peoples. Their emphasis is on the repeatability we observe, for example, with the beginning of each year. By returning to the point of origin of the world, the cosmogony, the time of the gods and the presence of their power is reestablished. To be sure, people who live with such an understanding of what is significant still have an awareness of the linear passingness of time. They know that they grow older, change, and move toward death. But what significantly organizes their world is the time of the beginnings, which recurs cyclically.

Judaism and Christianity, on the other hand, emphasize the historicity of time. The creation occurred in the beginning; later along the line of history Moses received the law, and the covenant was established; and for the Christian tradition, still later on this line Jesus Christ came into history. It is within history that God reveals himself to human beings. The line is actually an arrow; it is going in a direction that is planned by God and will end with the coming of the Messiah for Jews and the Parousia, Second Coming, for Christians. But we must remember that even with this emphasis on historical, linear time, both the Jewish and Christian traditions also incorporate cyclical time as, through ritual, one is able to reenact in mythic time, *in the present moment,* what occurred *once* in historical time.

Time is also an essential part of any literary work. Literature is an art that must involve the passage of time for its apprehension. It is made up of words, and words unfold one after the other in succession, in time. Although none of our apprehensions takes place out of time, we can make a practical distinction between the linear arts of literature and music and the spatial arts of sculpture and painting. A sculpture presents itself to us at once. Although we may spend time contemplating it, it is there in its wholeness from the first. With both music and literature the work must unfold in time, note after note, word after word. Our apprehension of wholeness comes only after we have finished reading the succession of words and see in retrospect how they form a completed pattern of meaning. We could say from the Judeo-Christian view that our willingness to move from word to word, anticipating and trusting that a pattern will emerge, is possible because we understand the moments of time in history to be moving meaningfully toward a goal that will reveal the pattern into which every event fits.

Deuteronomic View of History

One expression of this understanding of history in the Bible is called the Deuteronomic view of history. It is found primarily in the book of Deuteronomy and in the Prophets. Simply stated, it holds that Yahweh acts in history by making a covenant with the Hebrew people. When they keep their part of the bargain, God rewards them with peace and prosperity. However, when they fall away from the covenant, God punishes them by bringing on disasters, such as the invasion of the Assyrians or their captivity by the Babylonians, in order to bring them back to himself. History has a goal and God is directing its fulfillment by the rewards and punishments he gives to the Hebrew people.

However, there has occurred in the contemporary world an event that makes it difficult for many Jews to affirm the Deuteronomic view of history. If the disasters that occurred to the Jews are the punishment by Yahweh for their failure to observe the covenant, then Hitler was used by God to destroy six million Jews in the Nazi death camps. Richard Rubenstein, a contemporary Jewish theologian, tries to meet this question head on in his book *After Auschwitz*. He describes a conversation he had with a German Christian minister:

> For the pastors the conviction remained . . . that nowhere in the world were the fruits of God's activity in history more evident than in the life

and the destiny of the Jewish people. In each instance I very quickly rejoined that such thinking has as its inescapable conclusion the conviction that the Nazi slaughter of the Jews was somehow God's will, that God really wanted the Jewish People to be exterminated. . . .

Dr. Grüber arose from his chair and rather dramatically removed a Bible from a bookcase, opened it and read: ". . . for Thy sake are we slaughtered every day . . ." (Ps. 44:22). . . .

When Dr. Grüber put down his Bible, it seemed as if, once having started, he could not stop himself. He looked at recent events from a thoroughly Biblical perspective. In the past, the Jews had been smitten by Nebuchadnezzar and other "rods of God's anger." Hitler was simply another such rod. The incongruity of Hitler as an instrument of God never seemed to occur to him.[38]

Rubenstein goes on to point out the seeming injustice of this being God's punishment because the most religious Jews, the Hasidic communities in Poland, were the most thoroughly ravaged. However, this further explanation is usually unnecessary. No matter what the sin of the people who were killed, it is difficult for many people to understand the death camps through the Deuteronomic view of history. Rubenstein's response to this event is to propose an end to history and the God of history. He suggests an understanding of God as the God of nature, and thus he solves this dilemma by moving to a cyclical view of time. He sees the establishment of the state of Israel and the return to the land with its cycles of death and rebirth as the preeminent example of this new emphasis on the nonhistorical side of the Hebrew tradition.

Emil Fackenheim, in his remarkable book *God's Presence in History,* suggests another possibility—one that does not ignore the realities of evil and suffering in the world but nonetheless affirms the active presence of God in history.

While Auschwitz is new, evil in history is not. Thus Jeremiah protests against the prosperity of the wicked (Jer. 12:1)—and receives no answer. Job protests against his own undeserved suffering. . . . To give still a third example, when Jerusalem was destroyed by the Romans the rabbis could see no meaning in the event. Yet in all three cases—and in countless others—Jewish faith not only refused to despair of God, it also refused to disconnect Him with history and to seek escape in mysticism or otherworldliness.[39]

Nevertheless, Fackenheim clearly realizes the horrors of Auschwitz and the difficulty of understanding the meaning of God's presence in that historical event.

[38]Richard L. Rubenstein, *After Auschwitz: Radical Theology and Contemporary Judaism* (Indianapolis: Bobbs-Merrill, 1966), pp. 52–54.

[39]Emil L. Fackenheim, *God's Presence in History: Jewish Affirmations and Philosophical Reflections* (New York: Harper & Row, 1972), p. 7.

He begins by going back to the "root" experiences of Judaism, which reveal there has always been a dialectic in Jewish experience between the transcendence of God and his involvement in history; the power of God and the reality of human freedom; and the divine involvement with history and the evil within it.[40] What is experienced in the root experiences through these seeming contradictions is the saving presence of God (as at the Red Sea with the redemption from Egypt) and the commanding presence of God (as at Mt. Sinai with the giving of the Law). And, Fackenheim asserts, the saving and commanding presence of God is felt still at Auschwitz. The saving presence, however, is hidden; what remains for us is the commanding voice of Auschwitz. Jews are commanded not to forget the events of the death camps but to remember and to tell the story so the world will also not forget. Jews are commanded to survive—and to survive as Jews—in order not to continue the work begun by Hitler. Jews are commanded to continue to hope and to bear witness to that hope to the nations. Finally, Jews are commanded to continue to wrestle with God.

> The ways of the religious Jew are revolutionary, for there is no previous Jewish protest against divine Power like his protest. Continuing to hear the Voice of Sinai as he hears the Voice of Auschwitz, his citing of God against God may have to assume extremes which dwarf those of Abraham, Jeremiah, Job, Rabbi Levi Yitzhak. (You have abandoned the covenant? We shall not abandon it! You no longer want Jews to survive? We shall survive, as better, more faithful, more pious Jews! You have destroyed all grounds for hope? We shall obey the commandment to hope which You Yourself have given!) . . . For the religious Jew, who remains within the Midrashic framework, the Voice of Auschwitz manifests a divine Presence which, as it were, is shorn of all except commanding Power. This Power, however, is inescapable.
>
> No less inescapable is this Power for the secularist Jew who has all along been outside the Midrashic framework and this despite the fact that the Voice of Auschwitz does not enable him to return into that framework. He cannot return; but neither may he turn the Voice of Auschwitz against that of Sinai. For he may not cut off his secular present from the religious past: the Voice of Auschwitz commands preservation of that past. Nor may he widen the chasm between himself and the religious Jew: the Voice of Auschwitz commands Jewish unity.[41]

Although Rubenstein and Fackenheim respond in very different ways to the events of the death camps, each feels it is necessary

[40]Ibid., p. 17.
[41]Ibid., pp. 88–89.

to struggle with the meaning of history in light of their religious tradition.

In the literature of the modern period we find a complementary struggle with history. There seems to be an obsession with time in this literature. It often becomes the subject of literary works, and it is usually the cause of outrage or despair. In James Joyce's *Ulysses,* Stephen Dedalus says, "History . . . is a nightmare from which I am trying to awake."[42] The theory of relativity that was developed in the sciences often receives expression in other aspects of life as change without meaning. This, along with the loss of a religious framework that united all aspects of life as parts of a meaningful pattern in history, has led to a terror of time. It is time that brings change, destroys unity, leads to death. History is seen as one minute following another, with no meaningful connection between them. Thus, much of the art of the modern period that has been concerned with time has tried to escape from the meaninglessness of history. Without the God of history to ensure a meaningful pattern and direction to the passage of time, time can only destroy.

Wiesel's Struggle with the God of History

Elie Wiesel has faced the question of the Deuteronomic view of history in fiction. His autobiographical novel *Night* describes the experiences of a Jewish community in Poland through the eyes of a fourteen year old boy. He and his family and friends are taken prisoner by the Germans and transported to concentration camps, including Auschwitz, where most of them die. This child survives to tell the story, and the story he tells is the experience Wiesel himself went through.

As the novel begins, before the arrival of the Germans, we see that time is marked by the religious rituals of the Jewish year. Passover, Pentecost—these events are the way of organizing one's time and one's life. Even after they are taken to the camps many of the rituals continue to be observed. Rosh Hashana and Yom Kippur are celebrated; but, for the narrator at least, the "celebration" of these events, and so of the God of history, becomes a torment. He experiences in himself and in others around him in the camp the turning away from concern for other people and a turning inward into emptiness. The primary concern becomes food and temporary safety. And it is food for oneself and one's own

---

[42]James Joyce, *Ulysses* (New York: Random House, 1934), p. 35.

safety that take priority. The dead are quickly forgotten or go unmourned entirely. We do discover some instances of care for others and risking one's own food or life for another, but these are exceptions in the dark world of the camp. So there is no sense of celebration. For the narrator there is the added conflict that what is being celebrated in the religious rituals is the God of history. How can he praise the ways of Yahweh when the logic of tradition says that they have brought him into the death camps? His revolt against God begins:

> Some talked of God, of his mysterious ways, of the sins of the Jewish people, and of their future deliverance. But I had ceased to pray. How I sympathized with Job! I did not deny God's existence, but I doubted His absolute justice.[43]

On the eve of Rosh Hashana, the celebration of the New Year, his despair and outrage grow:

> In spite of everything, this day was different from any other. . . . Night was falling. Other prisoners continued to crowd in, from every block, able suddenly to conquer time and space and submit both to their will. . . .
> "Blessed be the Name of the Eternal!"
> Why, but why should I bless Him? In every fiber I rebelled. Because He had had thousands of children burned in His pits? Because He kept six crematories working night and day, on Sundays and feast days? Because in His great might He had created Auschwitz, Birkenau, Buna, and so many factories of death? How could I say to Him: "Blessed art Thou, Eternal, Master of the Universe, Who chose us from among the races to be tortured day and night, to see our fathers, our mothers, our brothers, end in the crematory? Praised be Thy Holy Name, Thou Who hast chosen us to be butchered on Thine altar?" (Pp. 77–78)

Another view, equally despairing, is presented by the narrator as he is forced to observe the hanging of a young child.

> One day when we came back from work, we saw three gallows rearing up in the assembly place, three black crows. Roll call. SS all round us, machine guns trained: the traditional ceremony. Three victims in chains—and one of them, the little servant, the sad-eyed angel. . . .
> The three victims mounted together onto the chairs.
> The three necks were placed at the same moment within the nooses.
> "Long live liberty!" cried the two adults.
> But the child was silent.
> "Where is God? Where is He?" someone behind me asked.
> At a sign from the head of the camp, the three chairs tipped over.
> Total silence throughout the camp. On the horizon, the sun was setting.

---

[43]Elie Wiesel, *Night*, trans. Stella Rodway (New York: Avon Books, 1969), pp. 55–56. The following quotations are taken from this edition.

"Bare your heads!" yelled the head of the camp. His voice was raucous. We were weeping.
"Cover your heads!"
Then the march past began. The two adults were no longer alive. Their tongues hung swollen, blue-tinged. But the third rope was still moving; being so light, the child was still alive. . . .
For more than half an hour he stayed there, struggling between life and death, dying in slow agony under our eyes. And we had to look him full in the face. He was still alive when I passed in front of him. His tongue was still red, his eyes not yet glazed.
Behind me, I heard the same man asking:
"Where is God now?"
And I heard a voice within me answer him:
"Where is He? Here He is—He is hanging here on this gallows." (Pp. 75–76)

Wiesel reveals with brutal starkness the horrors of the death camps and the horrors in himself. Many times the only reason he goes on living is because of his father: to stay with him, to try to protect him. Yet he discovers that in his heart he longs to be rid of the burden of caring for someone else. At one point they become separated, and only the next morning does he even remember to look for him. But he says, even as he looks, "'Don't let me find him! If only I could get rid of this dead weight, so that I could use all my strength to struggle for my own survival, and only worry about myself.' Immediately I felt ashamed of myself, ashamed forever" (p. 118).

In this dark world of the death camps Wiesel experiences betrayal. He feels betrayed by God—the God of history—but he also knows that he betrays not only God and his religious tradition but also his father, whom he longs to be rid of, and his mother and sister, whom he even forgets to worry about (and whom he never sees again). The darkness is overwhelming. We experience history that has ceased to have meaning or perhaps has acquired a demonic direction. There are fleeting glimpses of human solidarity reaching for something beyond the human; but Wiesel's story, as that of many of the prophets of the Old Testament, is one of doom. Unlike the prophets of the ancient Hebraic tradition, however, Wiesel cannot point to the promises of the God of history. He can only tell the story.

Art and History

We have seen another example of this struggle with history in Sartre's *Nausea*. Contingency—the lack of necessity for anything to be or for any event to occur—means that time has no meaning.

Another writer who explores the question of meaning in history is Ralph Ellison. In *Invisible Man* Ellison presents a black man's search for a meaningful way to act in history. He tries playing by the rules of a racist system; he tries joining the forces that oppose this system. But in everything he does he discovers that he is being used for ends opposite to those for which he was working. Every action he takes that he believes to be meaningful ends up being demonic. He finally comes to the point of questioning the possibility of any meaningful action because of the basic meaninglessness of history. His whole structure for organizing reality begins to fall apart as he questions, "What if history was a gambler, instead of a force in a laboratory experiment? . . . What if history was not a reasonable citizen, but a madman full of paranoid guile?"[44] If history cannot be trusted to provide a meaningful order, there is only chaos and invisibility.

In both Sartre and Ellison there is the suggestion that some meaningful order might be possible through the creative design of art. Roquentin found meaning in music and proposes to write a novel. This is the one action he feels he can take that will have meaning. Although we do not know if he writes the novel, we do have the record of his diary, which is the novel Sartre has written. In *Invisible Man* the nameless protagonist writes his experiences of struggling with history. The novel is in the form of his recounting all that has happened to him. At the end of the novel he is prepared to go into the world to try again, even though his actions have proved futile so many times before. He has learned that what he can do is tell his story. This is an action that is meaningful. And in the telling of it—through the ordering process of art—he comes to understand the experiences he has had and to discover that he must accept the chaos with the pattern and go on acting even though the chaos is never overcome. In this discovery he chooses to affirm history and to act within it in a way that Roquentin does not. For the protagonist of *Nausea,* art is a way of escaping from history, from time. For the Invisible Man it provides a way of reentering, reaffirming, and trusting the historical process that is closer to the Judeo-Christian understanding of time. Wiesel comes to a similar point as he discovers that he can and must tell the story. In chapter six we will explore further the religious power of storytelling.

---

[44]Ralph Ellison, *Invisible Man* (New York: Random House, 1972), p. 333.

THEOLOGY AND LITERATURE

We have traversed a very large territory as we have discussed religious themes that might receive expression in works of art. We could go into much greater detail about each of these. We could find many modern novels that share the concerns of these religious themes and symbols and might be either in continuity or discontinuity with them. And there are, of course, countless other symbols and themes from the Judeo-Christian tradition or other religious traditions we might also examine and use in our discussion of religious dimensions of works of art. What we have done to this point is establish a way in which we can talk about religious themes and symbols in relation to literature.

It should be noted again that religion and literature are two different things. We cannot equate literature with theological doctrine. Nor can we equate religion with aesthetic experience. We do not wish to make one into the other. Rather we *do* wish to enrich our understanding of each through our study of them together. As we approach a work of art, we look closely at what is there. We try not to impose our theological categories on it. Rather, we try to let the work of art reveal what it has to say. We take Joyce Cary's advice and examine with care all the contours of the work to see what patterns emerge. We may then discuss these patterns the work has presented to us in relation to a religious symbol, theme, or theological idea that shares the same concerns as the work of art. We may wish at this point to judge how closely the literary symbol agrees with the religious symbol, we may be able to see in the work new symbolic manifestations and transformations of tradition. The work of art may then open for us a new understanding of the religious symbol as it presents it in a way that is available within the context of contemporary culture. And the religious symbol or theological idea may enrich our reading of the novel as it expresses within the larger religious tradition the concerns shared by the particular work of art.

We will continue our discussion of religious dimensions of literature in the following chapters by exploring literature as possibility, literature as dialogue, and literature as mythopoesis. In each case, however, it will still be important to take care not to impose our theological categories on the work but to look closely at what it has to reveal to us. Our hope in each case will be a mutual enrichment of the literature and religion, which may in turn lead to a greater understanding on our part of the religious dimensions of our culture.

Chapter Five
LITERATURE AS POSSIBILITY

The storyteller begins, "Once upon a time," and we are drawn into a world of possibility. The artist uses the materials of our everyday world to create a hypothetical world, a world of "as if." Our imagination responds to these creations, and we are able to entertain the possibilities they reveal. We catch a glimpse not of what is but of what might be. The language of religion is also the language of possibility. The "more than" of religious experience thrusts itself into our everyday world, calling us not to what is, but to what might be.

Possibility in both literature and religion is closely related to the power of language to connect our immediate, actual reality with the not-yet-realized, but possible, realities that surround us. In this chapter we will explore this power of language and the imagination as it is revealed in literature and religion.

LITERATURE AS A HYPOTHETICAL CREATION

A writer asks us to suspend our ordinary categories of judgment and to enter into the world of artistic creation. As Giles Gunn puts it, "Every work of literature argues implicitly, whether it is a poem, novel, or play, 'If you will grant me my initial premise or set of conditions, then such and such would, or at least could, follow from them.'"[1] He agrees with Roy Harvey Pearce in asserting that a work of art is not literally "true," but

---

[1] Giles B. Gunn, "Introduction: Literature and Its Relation to Religion," *Literature and Religion*, ed., Giles B. Gunn (New York: Harper & Row Publishers, 1971), p. 23. A later version of this essay appears as chap. 2 of *The Interpretation of Otherness: Literature, Religion and the American Imagination*, Giles Gunn (New York: Oxford University Press, 1979).

consists instead of a series of hypothetical situations, imaged and moti-
vated in such a way that, within their confines, we can accept as necessary
the actions and responses into which the situations—and the imagined
human beings in them—are made to issue. What primarily interests us in
"created" situations of this sort is, of course, not their inevitable
relevance to factuality, but their possibility: their resonance with our
deepest sense of ourselves.[2]

We do not judge a work of art by its trueness to the everyday
world in which we live, but we "suspend our disbelief," enter into
its own logic, and judge it by its trueness to its own reality—its
consistency of character, action, and idea. We give what Pearce
calls "as-if assent" as we enter into the world of a work of art. We
do not expect to encounter our everyday world; and if it does
resemble our own reality, it is a reality transformed by the
possibilities of art. In twentieth century art, for example, Salvador
Dali's *Autumn Cannibalism* is hardly a scene one would expect to
see in one's backyard. On the other hand, we would expect to see
Andy Warhol's *Campbell's Soup Can* on a kitchen shelf rather than
in a museum of art. In both cases the artists are asking for our as-
if assent as they take us into a world of their own creation.

We must now ask, however, is there *no* relation between the
world of a work of art and the world in which we live? How can it
mean anything to us if it is unrelated to what we know to be
reality? And further, why should we care about it if the aesthetic
experience has nothing to do with our lived experience of everyday? If the possibilities that a world of art presents are unrelated to
what we know to be actual, they can have no meaning or significance for us.

In order for our imagination to entertain something new as a
possibility, it must have some connection with what we know
through our experience of the world. The materials of the hypothetical creation that is called art are the materials of the world that
we know. They are selected, organized, and transformed in a way
that is not common to lived experience, but they are not discon-
tinuous with lived experience. Giles Gunn states:

> [The artist's] capacity to see in the realities we all know hidden possibi-
> lities and potentialities we never dreamed of would not remain convincing
> to us if it were not based upon his and our knowledge of what apparently
> or most probably is. The sequence or structure of possibility, which at its
> most abstract defines the form of his work, must ultimately seem, if not

---

[2]Gunn, "Introduction," p. 24, quoting Roy Harvey Pearce, "Historicism Once
More," *The Kenyon Review* 20 (Autumn 1958): 566.

altogether natural and inevitable, at least plausible and compelling to "our deepest sense of ourselves."[3]

The artist arranges these materials in such a manner that they form a coherent, integrated world. Within this world one finds characters who have definite, consistent personalities, whose actions are attributable to discernable motivations, whose thoughts and speech are in accord with their total personalities. But we cannot stop with the characters themselves. We must add that all these things are true within the larger world of the work of which these characters are a part. A character's actions may seem to be inconsistent or unmotivated in themselves (and to the other characters who perceive them), but in terms of the larger frame of the work the inconsistency makes sense to us. This raises the question of how we are to know when we should take a character's actions or thoughts as illuminating the ordering principle of the world—i.e., when we should accept his or her words or actions as revealing the truth of the world the artist has created and when we should stand aside and see the character as failing to see something about the order of the world that we do see. One way of putting this question is to ask whose point of view we accept as normative for the world this artist has created. Where do we look to discover the values and beliefs that hold this hypothetical world together? in one of the characters? in the narrator? in the more subtle nuances by which a writer lets us understand the work of art? Much of this, of course, is done without any deliberate analysis. We usually know immediately which characters we are to sympathize with and trust and which we are to see as destructive. The writer leads us to accept the values and beliefs of the world by revealing to us what is to be affirmed and what denied. We are asked to accept a particular point of view toward reality and to entertain the possibilities that such a view would allow.

To discover the point of view and so the possibilities that the novel reveals, we must examine the plot, which is the imitation of an action according to Aristotle's *Poetics*. The word "imitation" stresses the hypothetical character of the world of art. "Action" stresses the importance of the incidents, through which the characters act and speak. This action, as a whole and in its individual parts, is directed toward an end, which for Aristotle is moral. This end we have called the organizing principle of a work. It is what gives the work of art unity and wholeness. There is nothing in a novel or a poem or a painting that is superfluous. Everything is there for a purpose; everything serves an end—it is this that

[3]Ibid., p. 24.

makes a work of art a work of art. There is unity; there is a point of view; there is a system of values and beliefs that provide coherence and order and reveal to us possibilities of what is not, but what might be, in our world.

An interesting thing to note is that, generally speaking, our world does not possess the unity, wholeness, and coherence that we have ascribed to a work of art. There is much we do and much we observe in everyday living that seem incidental or superfluous. As far as I can see, as I make my way through a day, not everything that occurs, either within me or beyond me, is relevant to the "plot." There are unnecessary details; there is a haphazardness no artist would allow. One way of defining art is, of course, just this: it is a process of selection and interpretation that gives a work of art a coherence and completeness not found in life. However, we must also note that one of the functions of a religious view of existence is to provide just such a coherent pattern to the events of daily living. Thus, through the hypothetical creation that is the work of art we see what it would be like to live within such a world, and we see, as well, the analogous relationship that exists between an artistic creation and a religious understanding of the world. This "as if" experience may not only expand the horizons of our actual experience and encourage us to new modes of action in the world, but it may also recall us to the possibility of a religious "story" that orders our world and gives meaning to our lives.

We see a further analogy with religious experience when we look at the system of values and beliefs that lies at the heart of the work of art and reveals its unity and wholeness to us. Giles Gunn describes the analogous relationship between these beliefs and values and the "religious experience of reality as ultimate":

> Every work of imaginative literature is based upon some deeply felt, if not fully or even partially conscious, assumption about what can, or just possibly does, constitute the ground of experience itself. This primal intuition then becomes the organizing principle for the hypothetical structure which the work turns out to be. And because this intuition or assumption thus undergirds and conditions all that transpires within the world of the work, it in turn becomes the interpretive key which will unlock the work's special logic, its peculiar causality, and thus lay bare the axis upon which the world of the work turns. Call it what you will—the informing or presiding assumption, the shaping cause, the concrete universal, the embodied vision, or the metaphysic—every meaningfully coherent work of literature has such an executive principle, and it functions analogously to the notion of ultimacy in religious experience.[4]

In this crucial statement about the possibilities of exploring religious dimensions of literature, Gunn provides us with a working definition of religion; he describes how we can get at the organizing principle of a work and so gives us a principle of interpretation; and he postulates the connection between aesthetic experience and religious experience. We will look now at the importance of possibility in religious experience itself and then explore further the analogous connection between these two aspects of human experience.

POSSIBILITY IN RELIGIOUS EXPERIENCE

The concept of possibility is important in many definitions of religious experience. Religion as the "Something More" of human existence indicates the sense of possibility, of something we cannot wholly grasp, which nonetheless promises transformation. Religion as the "means of ultimate transformation" carries this promise of a new becoming, of new possibilities that, according to van der Leeuw, we can never fully understand. They remain the "beyond," the "farthest boundary," which beckons us beyond what we now are and know. The phrase "Wholly Other" also implies an abundance we can never know or be, but in its otherness—which we as humans can imagine only as possibility—it has the power to transform who we are. Our response to these different formulations of the ultimate has been described as astonishment. The newness, the possibility we had not imagined, catches us by surprise. In Otto's terms we respond to the mystery—the ultimate possibility—of the sacred with awe and fascination. Both terms evoke the sense of standing in a Presence that remains a mystery, remains concealed, but also discloses possibilities before unimagined, which make all the difference in what it means to exist in this world.

We can see, then, that possibility is an important part of much of the language we use when we approach the sacred. It is because the ultimate is something other than what we as humans are and because it promises something more we may become that it has the character of sacredness. And this otherness and promise present us with possibilities of what is not but of what might be.

Within the Christian tradition, possibility is also very important. In the Gospel of Luke, Jesus begins his ministry in Nazareth by reading from the prophet Isaiah:

> The Spirit of the Lord is upon me, because he has anointed me to preach good news to the poor. He has sent me to proclaim release to the captives

and recovering of sight to the blind, to set at liberty those who are oppressed, to proclaim the acceptable year of the Lord. (Luke 4:18–19)

Throughout his ministry Jesus promises transformation, newness of life. He looks at the way things are and he asserts the possibility of something more. He presents the vision of a new world through the coming of the Kingdom of God. In the parables of the Kingdom Jesus relates, we discover in almost every case this sense of newness, of possibility beyond what we now know. And in almost every parable of the Kingdom this newness comes as a surprise. It is not what we would have expected or could have anticipated. Van der Leeuw's term "astonishment" describes our response to Jesus' promises of the Kingdom. The Kingdom, Jesus says, is like a mustard seed, the smallest of seeds, which—incredibly—grows into a tree large enough for birds to nest in. If we understand the parable of the good Samaritan as a parable of the Kingdom, the surprise takes a slightly different form. The Samaritans were so shunned by the Jewish people that even to drink their water or to accept help from them was repugnant. The fact that lifesaving assistance should come to the Jew on the road to Jericho from this despised Samaritan was a surprise that would not have pleased the Jewish people. The Kingdom, the parable would then inform us, may not come in just the garb we had expected or hoped for. It comes as a possibility we had not even entertained.

We respond to this possibility beyond our imagining with faith—the acceptance of possibilities beyond the actualities we know. Faith is described as "the assurance of things hoped for, the conviction of things not seen" (Heb. 11:1). The possibility promised by Jesus is transformation and newness of life: "I came that they may have life, and have it abundantly" (John 10:10). In the time of transformation, God will be all in all. This abundance of life and presence of God in everything are promises that inform and direct the lives of believers, even while remaining possibilities that will be fully realized only with the Parousia.

This anticipation of what might be, which receives partial fulfillment in the present while continuing to point beyond it, is the final element of possibility we will consider. "Prolepsis" is the term used to describe this present anticipation of a future realization. Even though the full realization of the Kingdom of God is expected in the future (with the second coming of Christ), it is present by prolepsis now and as such it guides our actions *as if* it were already here. When Paul is describing the last supper shared by Jesus and his disciples he says, after repeating the words Jesus spoke over the bread and wine, "For as often as you eat this bread and drink the cup, you proclaim the Lord's death until he comes"

(I Cor. 11:26). In this proclamation is the promise of what is to come, and in the promise there is also an actualization of the possible in the present moment.

The importance of possibility in Christianity is explored by Jürgen Moltmann in his book *The Theology of Hope*. The hope he describes is predicated on the promises that are given by the God of the Judeo-Christian religion. "A promise is a declaration which announces the coming of a reality that does not yet exist."[5] This reality is not congruent with reality as it now is; "there always remains an overspill."[6] This overspill, this *more* of the promise, provides a lure into the future. The future promises a fulfillment that the present anticipates but can never fully realize. By hope in the promise we are moved forward toward that "horizon of possibility" that challenges reality as we know it and draws us forward to the not-yet of human existence.

We see this promise and hope in the Old Testament as Yahweh enters into a covenantal relationship with his people. He who is God and could do anything he chose, promises that he will be the God of the people Israel; and, if they will obey his commandments, he will bring them many blessings. These blessings are seen in terms of the land of Israel and the Messiah or the Messianic age when all God's blessings will be realized on earth. These two promises often went together in Jewish history; the return to the land of Palestine would signal the beginning of the Messianic age. In the New Testament, the promise is again presented in terms of a covenant, now a new covenant given through Jesus Christ. There is a realization of the promise: the Messiah has come, but there is also a promise for the future. The Christ will come again, ushering in the reign of God's Kingdom. In both cases, through God's engagement with human beings in a covenantal relationship, there is both something given and something promised. Because God is in relationship with us here and now and because he promises future blessings, it is possible to live in the present with trust and to anticipate the future with hope. Because of the promise that it is God's future that lies ahead, we can live toward that future, which is unknown and so involves risk, with confidence. We can be open to possibility and newness because the not-yet is affirmed as the promise of God.

---

[5]Jürgen Moltmann, *The Theology of Hope: On the Ground and the Implications of a Christian Eschatology,* trans. James W. Leitch (New York: Harper & Row, 1965), p. 103.

[6]Ibid., p. 105.

IMAGINATION AND LANGUAGE IN THE CREATION OF POSSIBILITY

In this section we will examine the contours of a world of possibility and the way this world can be expanded by works of the imagination. Language and imagination play a central and interrelated role in fashioning the boundaries of the world. It is through our imagination that we can envision what is not yet and entertain the possibility of what might be. Our imagination, as all our thinking, is necessarily related to our language. Language is the link between the hazy, undefined realm of potentiality and our ability to give form to that realm and, perhaps, to bring it to actuality in the world. We will consider these two subjects—imagination and language—in this section. We will also explore the forms these two facets of our experience take as we look at possibility in the contemporary world.

When we look at the world through the eyes of possibility, we discover a place in which newness and spontaneity dominate. What is is not determinative of what might be. We are invited to create something new and with each new creation a myriad of new possibilities for creation come into being. Our imagination and expectations are altered with each new achievement. The horizon of possibility is continually inviting us to move forward to new imaginings and new creations. A rather startling joy of creation is the process of continual becoming, the newness we encounter that occasions surprise and affirmation. This view affirms the world as a process of movement and change, growth and uniqueness. It is an affirmation of the ground of being as possibility.

We as human beings are able to enter and live in such a world because the power of the imagination allows us to be open to possibilities that are unlike our present reality. Gaston Bachelard says our imagination faces the future.[7] Our world is not bound or contained by what is known and accounted for. The future is not seen as a continuation of what has been. Rather, there is the promise of newness and transformation that lies ahead; and it is our capacity to imagine that allows us to move into this future. If we could know only what we know, if we could think only about what *is* (according to the boundaries of our knowledge of the world), then our world would be static; there could be nothing new for our understanding.

---

[7]Gaston Bachelard, *The Poetics of Space,* trans. Maria Jolas (Boston: Beacon Press, 1969), p. XXX.

Although we might readily affirm the importance of the imagination to the artist, we might be inclined to say, "Yes, but what of the scientist? The empirical method requires not imagination but the precise application of reason to the observation of what is. It is through this that the scientist may discover something new, not through the imagination." Although this is true to experimental procedures, we must ask, where does the scientist get the idea for an experiment? Is not creativity—and imagination—essential if the scientist is to carry out an experiment through which something new comes to be understood? Must not scientists be able to imagine what they do not know but which might possibly be the case if they are to extend the boundaries of our knowledge of the world?

When we view the world in such a way, acknowledging the fundamental importance of imagination and the fundamental structure of possibility, we are struck by the sense of mystery that pervades all our experiences of the world. We recognize that another person is not an object we can categorize and contain in a box. Rather, in that person, we sense the mystery of possibility we cannot grasp, but into whose presence we can come. The natural world also can no longer be understood as a collection of matter, operating machine-like by rules we can discover through our reason. There are rules but also more than rules. There is a mystery to life and to beings that constitutes a *presence* we can experience but cannot control. Gabriel Marcel says, "A presence can, in the last analysis, only be invoked or evoked, the evocation being fundamentally and essentially magical."[8] Through our imaginative capabilities we can call upon the "magic" that surrounds us in our world; and calling upon it through evoking it, we can enter into its presence and its power.

Imagination leads us into the mystery of the not-yet, the potentiality of existence. This potentiality can become incorporated into our being in the world, however, only as it takes on form. Experience must have a shape, a pattern, for us to perceive it and make it our own. Words are one way of providing this pattern. They enable us to experience and they give shape to our experience. Three diverse examples illustrate this point.

When I observe snow falling, I may differentiate between hail, frozen balls; sleet, frozen rain; and snow, something softer that comes in flakes. If, however, I lived in a land of snow—if I were

[8]Gabriel Marcel, *The Mystery of Being*, vol.1: *Reflection and Mystery* (Chicago: Henry Regnery Company, 1960), p. 256.

an Eskimo, for example—I would have a much larger number of words for "snow." And when I looked at a storm, I would not only be more discriminating in identifying the characteristics of the precipitations; I would also *see* it differently. Whether the perception is possible because of the words or whether the words have developed to meet the discriminating perceptions is difficult to say. Our experience of the world requires words, and words express our experience.

As a second example, George Orwell, in his novel *1984,* takes a more extreme position toward language. In the totalitarian world he constructs, the primary tool for ultimate domination of the very souls of people is control of language. The language of Oceania (which is one of the three powers in the world and includes what used to be England and the United States) is Newspeak. The goal of Newspeak is to eliminate as many words as possible from the dictionary. If there were no words for certain concepts, those concepts would cease to exist. The following statement is made by a person who is working on the new language—and approving it wholeheartedly:

> Don't you see that the whole aim of Newspeak is to narrow the range of thought? In the end we shall make thoughtcrime literally impossible, because there will be no words in which to express it. Every concept that can ever be needed will be expressed by exactly *one* word, with its meaning rigidly defined and all its subsidiary meanings rubbed out and forgotten. . . . Even now, of course, there's no reason or excuse for committing thoughtcrime. It's merely a question of self-discipline, reality-control. But in the end there won't be any need even for that. The Revolution will be complete when the language is perfect.[9]

When the word "freedom" no longer exists, for the generations who will never hear it, the reality and the possibility of freedom will also be nonexistent.

In addition to controlling language, the government also controls its people by regulating their memories. All books are rewritten to coincide with party policy. If a party member falls out of favor, all previous newspaper accounts of the person would be rewritten so that he was always a traitor—or he would be eliminated from all written accounts so that in history he never existed. And, without the written account and with bans against speaking of him, soon it would be as if he never were.

The final example is from the three major Western religious traditions. Within all of them the "word" is central. In Islam the

[9]George Orwell, *1984* (New York: New American Library, 1961), pp. 46–47.

word of Allah is recited to Muhammed and is called the Qur'ān, which means "recital." The speaking of this holy Scripture is the central ritual within this tradition. In Christianity Jesus Christ is known as the Word. The Gospel of John begins, "In the beginning was the Word, and the Word was with God, and the Word was God . . . and without him was not anything made that was made. . . . And the Word became flesh and dwelt among us" (John 1:1–3, 14). The Word made flesh is the Incarnation.

In Judaism the word is also of central significance. Yahweh gives his word to Moses at Sinai—the Written Torah and the Oral Torah—and it is the adherence to and study and interpretation of this word that form the core of Judaism. In the mystical traditions within Judaism the word takes on even greater importance. Here the words of Torah correspond to the structure of the universe. They are the human way of coming into contact with the ultimate dimensions of the cosmos. Tenakh, the Old Testament, is thus not just a historical account of the Hebrew people but reveals the very structure of the universe. In Hasidism as it developed in Judaism in the eighteenth century, the importance given to words is also revealed by its concern with storytelling. To tell the story is to cross the bridge of language that connects the human and divine. One of these stories is about the power of language, more particularly, the power of the alphabet, out of which words are composed. It is a story of Israel Baal Shem Tov, the founder of this movement, as retold by Elie Wiesel.

> And it came to pass that the great Rebbe Israel Baal Shem Tov, Master of the Good Name, known for his powers in heaven as well as on earth, decided to try once more to force his Creator's hand.
>
> He had tried many times before—and failed. Burning with impatience, he wanted to end the ordeals of exile forcibly; and this time he was but one step away from success. The gates were ajar; the Messiah was about to appear and console the children and old men awaiting him, awaiting no one else but him. The Diaspora had lasted long enough; now men everywhere would gather and rejoice.
>
> The heavens were in an uproar. The angels were dancing. Red with anger, outraged, Satan demanded an audience with God. Brought before Him, he protested, invoking laws and precedents, history and reason. Look at man's impudence, he said, how dare he take things into his own hands? Does the world deserve redemption? And the conditions to warrant the Messiah's coming, have they been met?
>
> God listened. And had to recognize the validity of Satan's arguments: *Lo ikhshar dara,* the Rebbe's gesture was judged premature; his generation was not yet ready for a miracle of such magnitude. Moreover, since the order of creation may not be disturbed with impunity, he and his faithful scribe Reb Tzvi-Hersh Soifer were deported to a distant uncharted island. Where they were promptly taken prisoners by a band of pirates.

Never had the Master been so submissive, so resigned.

"Master," the scribe pleaded, "do something, say something!"

"I can't," said the Baal Shem Tov, "my powers are gone."

"What about your secret knowledge, your divine gifts: your *yikhudim*? What happened to them?"

"Forgotten," said the Master. "Disappeared, vanished. All my knowledge has been taken away; I remember nothing."

But when he saw Hersh Soifer's despair, he was moved to pity. "Don't give up," he said, "we still have one chance. You are here, and that is good. For you can save us. There must be one thing I taught you that you remember. Anything—a parable, a prayer. Anything will do."

Unfortunately, the scribe too had forgotten everything. Like his Master, he was a man without memory.

"You really remember nothing," the Master asked again, "nothing at all?"

"Nothing, Master. Except . . ."

". . . except what?"

". . . the *aleph, beith."* (alphabet)

"Then what are you waiting for?" shouted the Master, suddenly excited. "Start reciting! Right now!"

Obedient as always, the scribe proceeded to recite slowly, painfully, the first of the sacred letters which together contain all the mysteries of the entire universe: "*Aleph, beith, gimmel, daleth . . .*"

And the Master, impatiently, repeated after him: "*Aleph, beith, gimmel, daleth . . .*"

Then they started all over again, from the beginning. And their voices became stronger and clearer: *aleph, beith, gimmel, daleth . . .* until the Baal Shem became so entranced that he forgot who and where he was. When the Baal Shem was in such ecstasy, nothing could resist him, that is well known. Oblivious to the world, he transcended the laws of time and geography. He broke the chains and revoked the curse: Master and scribe found themselves back home, unharmed, richer, wiser and more nostalgic than ever before.

The Messiah had not come.[10]

In each example the power of words is clearly expressed. Our experience of the world is bound up with our language. Through the interaction of words and experiences we are able to enter the realm of new possibilities and to evoke the magical presences, as Marcel says, which lead us to the "more" of human existence.

Possibility and the Contemporary World

What does possibility tell us about the world we live in and the manifestations of religion in our culture? There is no question that possibility is a basic constituent of our experience of the world. We seem sometimes, in fact, to be besieged by possibility.

[10]Elie Wiesel, *Souls on Fire: Portraits and Legends of Hasidic Masters,* trans. Marion Wiesel (New York: Random House, 1973), pp. 3–5.

People living in the contemporary world often long for certainty. We often think we would prefer a world that was less open to newness because it would be simpler, it would be more secure. Our experience is not of absolutes that stay in place but rather of a changing, unfolding reality that offers possibility but withholds certainty.

Our experience of the world has its counterpart in the scientific and philosophical understanding of our time. We know the world through interpretation. There is a dialectical interaction between our imagination and language on the one hand and the givenness of things on the other. But the "givenness" is not absolute. There is not one "reality" we can know in itself. We know things as they exist in relation to us as we perceive them, and we perceive them from a certain frame of reference. The relational character of our understanding of existence means we affect what we observe. In order to observe a subatomic particle, for example, we must interact with it (bombard it with a quantum of light); and, thus, what we can observe is the electron in relation to ourselves. We can never have the knowledge of the isolated electron as it exists in itself. Niels Bohr understands the uncertainty we must have regarding the actual working of the electron as being due to our limited conceptual tools. It is, in other words, uncertainty based on our inability to know.

Werner Heisenberg understands the uncertainty to be a matter not of what we can know (epistemology) but rather of the nature of reality itself (ontology). The Uncertainty or Indeterminacy Principle states that we cannot attribute causal determination to the subatomic world. We cannot expect electrons to behave according to our notions of cause and effect. There is a *randomness* found at this level. This does not mean that atomic events are uncaused but rather that they are not strictly determined. Therefore, when we observe this world, we disturb this "potentiality" by causing *one* of the possibilities to actualize itself.

This principle is interpreted to mean that there is built into the structure of existence, at the most basic level, the reality of potentiality or possibility. Thus we have moved away from the Newtonian causality that leads to a deterministic view of the natural (material) world. As Ian Barbour describes it, "The future is not simply unknown, it is 'not decided'; but it is not completely 'open,' since the present determines the range of future possibilities."[11]

[11]Ian G. Barbour, *Issues in Science and Religion* (Englewood Cliffs, N.J.: Prentice-Hall, 1966), pp. 304-5.

Alfred North Whitehead stresses both relation and possibility in his process philosophy. "Our whole experience is composed out of our relationships to the rest of things, and of the formation of new relationships constitutive of things to come. The present receives the past and builds the future."[12] Whitehead points out that the Newtonian and Cartesian world views see matter as distinct from the "I" who does the understanding. Although contemporary science demonstrates that these ideas are an inaccurate description of our world, Whitehead believes they are still the presuppositions by which we live. Things exist in space, and they are out there, unrelated to us.

It is no doubt a convenient abstraction for us to see a chair or a rock or a body as solid, as not involved in a process of change. But it is vital for understanding our being in the world to realize that in fact matter (a rock, e.g.) is composed of particles of energy that are constantly in process just as we are. Whitehead describes this process as the continual emergence of novelty. New creations, which he calls "actual occasions" (events being the fundamental units of reality), occur at every level of actuality, organic and inorganic. An actual occasion is not, of course, a stopping point, but becomes the material out of which new actual occasions come into being.

At the level of human beings this newness takes on a special form. We can entertain unrealized possibilities and look forward to their realization. Whitehead says we can define human beings by their sense of the importance of novelty. We are always aiming at the future, at the not-yet. The future is not determined but is formed by our interaction with the world.

Whitehead uses the term "causal efficacy" to describe the internal relations between events that move them into the future toward greater achievements of harmony and satisfaction. This is parallel to Barbour's discussion of indeterminacy and the future. In both cases causation in the usual sense of the word is not present. For Whitehead there is a meaningful connection between all events. However, the experience of our time is often to see the same evidence as destructive of all meaning. If there is an openness and indeterminacy at all levels of reality and if no exact causal connection exists between observable human events and experiences, then is it possible to talk about any meaningful connection between events? Or have we returned to Sartre's world of absolute contingency (see chapter four)?

[12]Alfred North Whitehead, *Modes of Thought* (New York: Free Press, 1968) p. 43.

In *The Crying of Lot 49* Thomas Pynchon raises this question in a way that parallels the scientific understandings of Bohr and Heisenberg and the philosophical ideas of Whitehead. The main character, Oedipa Maas, finds herself thrown into a world of mystery and danger when she is named executrix of the estate of an eccentric lover from her past, Pierce Inverarity. At the beginning of the novel she is a conservative, suburban housewife; but a part of her, which she usually hides from herself, senses that she is a prisoner of the life she is leading. She thought she had had an experience of something else with Pierce Inverarity; but she came to believe that with him, too, she remained trapped, a prisoner in a tower that was keeping her from reality. A painting she saw when she was in Mexico with Pierce becomes a metaphor for her perception of reality:

> In the central painting of a triptych, titled "Bordando el Manto Terrestre," were a number of frail girls with heart-shaped faces, huge eyes, spun-gold hair, prisoners in the top room of a circular tower, embroidering a kind of tapestry which spilled out the slit windows and into a void, seeking hopelessly to fill the void: for all the other buildings and creatures, all the waves, ships and forests of the earth were contained in this tapestry, and the tapestry was the world.[13]

When Oedipa leaves her Northern California suburban home and enters into the strange world of San Narcisco near Los Angeles to begin unraveling the estate, it *may be* that she has finally left her tower and is encountering real novelty and is involved both in the creation and the discovery of new possibilities. Or it may be she is still solipsistically weaving her own tapestry or playing her part in one that has been woven by another. The ambiguity of the experiences that await her is revealed in her first view of San Narcisco. As she looks down at the sprawl of houses and streets she thinks of the printed circuit of a transistor radio she had once seen.

> There'd seemed no limit to what the printed circuit could have told her (if she had tried to find out); so in her first minute of San Narcisco, a revelation also trembled just past the threshold of her understanding. Smog hung all round the horizon, the sun on the bright beige countryside was painful; she and the Chevy seemed parked at the centre of an odd, religious instant. As if, on some other frequency, or out of the eye of some whirlwind rotating too slow for her heated skin even to feel the centrifugal coolness of, words were being spoken. She suspected that much. (P. 13)

[13]Thomas Pynchon, *The Crying of Lot 49* (New York: Bantam Books, 1967), p. 10. The following quotations are taken from this edition.

Such words as "seemed," "as if," and "suspected" set the tenor for the whole novel. It *may be* that she is encountering revelations of new possibilities, but *certainty* always lies beyond her grasp.

As she begins her job as executrix a number of coincidences begin piling up, all of which seem to connect an underground postal system, dating back to the fourteenth century, with Inverarity's estate. She begins to see the symbol for the postal system as well as its acronym, WASTE (We Await Silent Tristero's Empire), everywhere, connecting and perhaps bringing together the most diverse sorts of people. And it seems they are withholding information from her and perhaps even threatening her life as she begins to put a variety of facts, symbols, events, and people together in a way that might link them all in some great conspiracy. It gets to the point where everything she perceives *seems* to fit together. Or does it? It seems either *everything* is related or *nothing* is related; there is either total determinacy or there is no causal efficacy between events but only meaningless coincidence. In trying to understand the apparent connectedness she sees around her, she decides there are four possible explanations:

> Either you have stumbled indeed . . . onto a secret richness and concealed density of dream; onto a network by which X number of Americans are truly communicating; . . . maybe even onto a real alternative to the exitlessness, to the absence of surprise to life, that harrows the head of everybody American you know, and you too, sweetie.(P. 128)

But this is only the first possibility—that there is something real and full of possibility. The others are that she is hallucinating or that a plot is being directed against her or that she is "fantasying some such plot, in which case you are a nut, Oedipa, out of your skull" (p. 128). She decides she would prefer the proper alternative be that she is crazy. Although the first possibility is full of promise, it is also full of great danger.

At another point, referring to all the signs and symbols that seem to present themselves to her, telling of a secret postal system linking all sorts of people in meaningful communication, she says, "Behind the hieroglyphic streets there would either be a transcendent meaning, or only the earth" (p. 136). She bemoans the fact that our world of choices has become like a digital computer—on/off, either/or—and indeed her experience seems to show that the options are (or may be) more complex than that.

In her wanderings she happens to meet Jesus Arrabal, a Mexican revolutionary she and Pierce had met in Mexico. He says to her, "You know what a miracle is. . . . Another world's intrusion into this one" (p. 88). It is precisely this sense of novelty and possibility that provides the hope and fear she feels as she seeks to uncover the mystery of Tristero. She looks at the America she knows—our America—and sees the apparent sham and pettiness and lack of communication. Yet she also looks at the clues that may be metaphors for a real system of communication—and, indeed, in her search she has come into relationship with any number of people. What she is left with, in a world of indeterminacy, is metaphor, which, she says, may be either a thrust at truth or a lie (p. 95); and she does not know which it is. To attempt to find out, to search for the something more, seems to pose great dangers and make great demands and may bring her to something she does not wish to find. But we see her at the end of the novel continuing her search, waiting for the next clue, the next symbol, which may mean everything . . . or nothing . . . or a miracle.

To approach our subject from a different angle let us consider how our frame of reference affects the way we view an event. Stephen Toulmin, in *Reason in Ethics,* describes the way in which we ask different questions to determine different things. For example, there are questions of science, of art, of religion. We cannot expect religion to answer the questions that science is equipped to deal with (explanation or prediction), nor can we expect science to take on questions suited to religion (meaning or purpose). He illustrates this in terms of science and art by describing an imagined conversation between an artist and a physicist as they walk together through a meadow and then through a wooded area. The artist exclaims, "The sky is a different color blue when seen through the trees!" The physicist answers, "No, the sky is not a different color. It just *looks* (or appears) that way." We might feel compelled to ask which person is *right*, the artist or the physicist? What color is the sky, *really?* Toulmin's response is that this is a meaningless question. There is no one right answer. Depending on the frame of reference one speaks from, the answer will be different. The physicist is concerned with predictability and for him the "real" color of an object does not change simply because we look at it through trees. If it did, we would not be able to predict. The artist, on the other hand, is not concerned with being able to predict what some future experience is going to be like. The pattern formed by the present experience is what is interesting. "He is not so much concerned to predict our future experiences as to record our present ones."[14] Therefore, looked at from the artist's perspective, the sky is really a deeper blue when seen through the trees. Looked at from the physicist's perspective it is really the same color blue. We cannot ask further than this, what color is it *really?*

Another example Toulmin uses from within science concerns Euclidian and non-Euclidian geometry as they are used in theoretical astronomy. In non-Euclidian geometry light rays are the standard of straightness and the astronomer will use this standard when talking about phenomena in outer space. However, at other times, for example, when talking about events occurring around the sun, the astronomer may speak of light rays being deflected. At this point the standard of straightness is no longer light rays (for if it were, they could not be bent or deflected); it is the standard of Euclidian geometry: the shortest distance between two points. It will do no good to ask the astronomer, "Well, is a light ray *really* straight or not?" There is no answer to this question without its context and without your frame of reference as you ask the question. If one is speaking from within Euclidian geometry, a light ray is not necessarily straight. If one uses non-Euclidian geometry as one's frame of reference, by definition a light ray is straight.[15]

Once again we find ourselves in that world of possibility, which is sometimes frightening, where things are not simply what they are. Wallace Stevens is a modern poet who has taken on a world with such contours, embraced it, and discovered within it potentiality— possibility—for endless creativity. In his poem "Thirteen Ways of Looking at a Blackbird" the multiplicity of reality is explored. The poem consists of thirteen short stanzas, each a single image in which the blackbird is present.

I
Among twenty snowy mountains,
The only moving thing

Was the eye of the blackbird.
II
I was of three minds,
Like a tree
In which there are three blackbirds.

---

[14]Stephen Edelston Toulmin, *An Examination of the Place of Reason in Ethics* (Cambridge: Cambridge University Press, 1960), pp. 113–14.
[15]Ibid., p. 110.

Depending on the stance or frame of reference one has, the blackbird is seen in a different way. This is not simply physical position, but psychological and spiritual as well. And the blackbird can never be exhausted by our descriptions of it—whether thirteen or one hundred. Reality for us depends on our perception of reality, not the blackbird alone, but as it is in relation to movement or time or mountains or our minds. It is within a context that we perceive the blackbird and possible contexts know no boundaries.

We also see in the poem, however, that just because we see things from different points of view that does not mean that they exist only in our minds or that we create them. There is a basis to our views, a givenness in the material of reality that is inescapable. The image of this givenness for Stevens, in the rather ominous symbolic form of the blackbird, casts a shadow over all contexts. The darkness of the bird, the association with death and with the shadow side of life, haunts all our relationships, our thoughts, the natural world. We see this in several other stanzas in the poem. The blackbird is present in all human relationships:

IV
A man and a woman
Are one.
A man and a woman and a blackbird
Are one.

We see it in the mysterious power of existence, in both its sound and its silence:

V
I do not know which to prefer,
The beauty of inflections
Or the beauty of innuendoes,
The blackbird whistling
Or just after.

Finally, the blackbird is associated with death and eternality. It is the limit on experience, the boundary that always remains:

XIII
It was evening all afternoon.
It was snowing
And it was going to snow.
The blackbird sat
In the cedar-limbs.[16]

---

[16]Wallace Stevens, *The Palm at the End of the Mind: Selected Poems and a Play,* ed. Holly Stevens (New York: Random House, Vintage Books Edition, 1972), pp. 20-22.

The blackbird is the presentness, the givenness of reality, but it is givenness as potentiality until it is apprehended and placed in a context, a pattern. And the ways of structuring reality are endless. Possibility must be actualized or structured for human beings to enter into it, and it is the role of the poet to present us with actualized patterns, which Stevens calls "supreme fictions." It is these patterns of meaning by which we live. He says in his prose work *The Necessary Angel*:

> There is . . . a world of poetry indistinguishable from the world in which we live, or, I ought to say, no doubt, from the world in which we shall come to live, since what makes the poet the potent figure that he is, or was, or ought to be, is that he creates the world to which we turn incessantly and without knowing it and that he gives to life the supreme fictions without which we are unable to conceive of it.[17]

This world is always filled with possibility as he says in his poem "An Ordinary Evening in New Haven":

> Reality is the beginning not the end,
> Naked Alpha, not the hierophant Omega. . . .
>
> It is the infant A standing on infant legs,
> Not twisted, stooping, polymathic Z. . . .
>
> Alpha continues to begin.
> Omega is refreshed at every end.

And further on:

> The poem is the cry of its occasion,
> Part of the res itself and not about it.[18]

In this "occasion" there is the actualization of possibility and the creation of new possibilities. The poem gives form to what it is a part of and, in doing so, makes it possible for us to conceive the potentialities of what is and what might be in the continual beginning of reality.

SCIENCE FICTION AND FANTASY AS FORMS OF POSSIBILITY

Possibility as an angle of vision for understanding literature in its religious dimension is obviously a part of every work of art insofar as art is a hypothetical creation. Whether a novel falls under the classification of "realism" or "fantasy," it offers an alternative world, a world that is not our own but which may

---

[17]Wallace Stevens, *The Necessary Angel: Essays on Reality and the Imagination* (New York: Random House, 1951), p. 31.
[18]Stevens, *Palm at the End of the Mind*, pp. 334–35.

resonate with our deepest sense of ourselves. Because we have the capacity for imagining, for entertaining the possibility of novelty, our experience of a hypothetical world can enter into our constant process of becoming.

In this section we will look at examples of the importance of possibility in the contemporary world through the literary forms of science fiction and fantasy. It is important to stress the fact that the meaning of possibility in these "non-realistic" forms is the same as in forms that appear to be more realistic depictions of our world. The difference may be that science fiction and fantasy, by creating worlds that appear significantly different from our own, refuse us the possibility of not acknowledging their hypothetical character.

Generally, fantasy creates a hypothetical world by pointing to a time in the past while science fiction points to a time in the future. The past in fantasy is the time of "once upon a time"; it is usually not located historically but takes us, instead, to prehistory when the laws we accept as maintaining our world were more open to mystery. Fantasy recalls the time when the gods—and beasts—walked the earth. If the work of fantasy is set in the modern period, we—and the characters—are struck by these mysterious presences in a world we had thought followed certain laws that excluded such powers. Science fiction, on the other hand, looks to the future when equally out-of-the-ordinary things may occur; but in this fiction they will be the result of science and technology rather than the work of fabulous creatures or gods. In both genres the world that is projected may be either a utopia—the time of a perfect society—or a dystopia—the time of the beasts in fantasy, the time of despotism and destruction in science fiction. In science fiction, however, the emphasis is on the human accomplishments or disasters that will be possible not by putting aside the "laws of nature" but through an extension of human powers to comprehend and manipulate them. In both cases this imagining of a time other than our time is not usually an escape from the present. Rather, both science fiction and fantasy are ways of exploring and revealing something about the present moment in which we live. The hope is not to escape either to the past or the future but, through an imaginative distancing from our present situation, to discover the meaning that lies within it.

Science Fiction and Our Futuristic Present

In *Structural Fabulation* Robert Scholes describes how literature of the future (science fiction) is particularly suited to the contemporary world. Scholes begins with the assumption that the crisis that is peculiar to our time (and each age, he does not doubt, has its own, equally significant crisis to confront and overcome) is the crisis of language. He asserts that our discovery has been that words and reality can never correspond. Our language is a symbol system, which gives us a model of reality (and there are any number of these models for interpreting reality: e.g., "Thirteen Ways . . .") rather than reality itself. Our language can never suffice to make the leap that connects our experience and our conceptualization. "Put simply, contemporary writers and critics have lost faith in the ability of language to correspond with the non-verbal parts of life."[19] Writers in the early part of the century, such as Joyce and Proust,

> shared a faith in the ability of their verbal art to give coherence to the actualities of the world around them. . . . But modern critics . . . have shown with devastating irony that even a great "realist" like Balzac did not make his linguistic code correspond with reality in-itself, but simply alluded in his language to other already codified beliefs, other codes which themselves inevitably lack genuine ontological status. Language is language and reality is reality—and never the twain shall meet.[20]

Nonetheless, it is not possible to dissociate fiction—a work of words—from reality. It can neither be equal to reality (the end of the old school of "realism"), nor can it be wholly divorced from what we know of reality (the end of a concept of "romance"). Rather it must work between these two, creating its own models, or structures, but models that are related to our lived experience. Scholes believes that in the contemporary world it is fiction of the future—science fiction—that is best able to mediate between these two realms.

He bases this understanding on an analysis of humankind's relationship to and understanding of time. He asserts that the earliest human beings began with the mythic, which he defines as an understanding of time that is cyclical and thus unchanging. Stories that are told in this time are stories of the beginnings, of how things came to be the way they are. The world reaches back to its origins rather than forward to a new future. With the historical view people understood their world in terms of a continuous process in which past and present were intimately related. It

---

[19]Robert Scholes, *Structural Fabulation: An Essay on Fiction of the Future* (Notre Dame: University of Notre Dame Press, 1975), p. 3.
[20]Ibid., p. 4.

was during this period that the novel as an imaginative form developed with a stress on the present and on realism. Scholes asserts that our present understanding of the world has moved beyond this historical approach to a *structural* approach. We concentrate not on the passage from one event to another but rather on the patterns or *gestalts* or systems that govern the cosmos as well as our social and psychological lives. In light of evolutionary and relativity theories the human measure that dominated the historical view is no longer adequate. Realism, which depends on a common sense approach to reality no longer serves when we become aware of the limitations of our common sense in light of such things as atoms and quarks and the space-time continuum. Thus, in Scholes's view, we have entered into a period in which we must come to discern the patterns that operate at all levels of our existence and to seek out the meanings that may grow from them. We are living in a world that necessitates interpretation, that is filled with possibilities out of which patterns must be discerned or created.

He believes that contemporary science fiction is especially suited to this time because there is no conflict between "realism" and the literature of science fiction. Language does not purport to describe reality, but rather a future possibility. It does this by providing possible structures that help us examine the patterns that give meaning to our lives. We may see the extension of our current patterns in the future and may, through this, see the dangers that lie ahead for us. Or we may see new patterns of possibility that may lead us to examine the present patterns we live by.

Science fiction has been called "speculative fiction" by Robert Heinlein, who is himself a master of this genre. It is speculative because it addresses itself to the future, suggesting possibilities of what lies ahead. It creates a "suspension of disbelief" in us by creating plausible worlds that are possible by extension. The devices and major themes of science fiction lend themselves to this speculation. For example, space travel allows us to enter worlds and societies other than our own, as well as to look back on our own earth from a different perspective. Time travel also enables us to move between different viewpoints and so, by contrast, to gain a clearer view of our own time. By a hypothetical extension of developments that are known to our time — e.g., computer technology and parapsychological ideas such as extrasensory perception — we are able to imagine where our present course may lead. It is sometimes portrayed as a totalitarian, mind-controlled society, sometimes as a creative civilization in which computers are used to solve the problems that plague us now and total communication through ESP removes the barriers that lead to conflict between people. Through these various ways of examining and living in a world different from our own, we are invited to speculate on the possibilities of what might be different about our lives in the present.

This chance to place ourselves imaginally in a different world through a story is, as we have said, the hallmark of all fiction, but it is less disguised in science fiction and fantasy. We will discuss storytelling in greater detail in the following chapter, but here let us note what Lois and Stephen Rose have to say about story in regard to science fiction:

> It is a merit of science fiction that it seeks to consider all possibilities within the potentially integrating reality of the story. . . . If the meaningful integration of our varied experiences is hard to come by these days, it is a measure of the loss of folktale and myth in our culture . . . . One function of the best sf is to restore to us the possibility of regaining a mythological penetration of our one-dimensional existence. If something can be *told*, it may participate in reality. If it is true that we literally *live* by stories, by myths in the almost lost sense of the term—tales that convey a reality that no other communicative device could contain—if we live in this way then the twin issues—nihilism versus hope, fantasy versus science—may be determined in . . . the telling of tales. By the refurbishing of our imaginations.[21]

Myth is understood here to be a way of telling the story of our beliefs and values. The Roses distinguish it from folktale by saying the latter tells the stories of a culture and its heroes in their victories; myth allows the ambiguities of human existence to be revealed. There is an element of tragedy in myth because of the irresolution of actual life. However, as our fragmentary experience is placed within the framework or structure of the mythic, story form, it gains a wholeness, a meaning, a *reality*. Bringing to language, then, through the forms of symbol, metaphor, and myth, is essential for the integration of our lives, both individually and as a community.

Science fiction, because it is not required to be representative of the real world as we know it, is able to create myths by literalizing the metaphors of our time.[22] This can show us either

---

[21]Lois and Stephen Rose, *The Shattered Ring: Science Fiction and the Quest for Meaning* (Richmond, Va.: John Knox Press, 1970), p. 28.

[22]See Robert M. Philmus, *Into the Unknown: The Evolution of Science Fiction from Francis Godwin to H. G. Wells* (Berkeley and Los Angeles: University of California Press, 1970), pp. 21-22.

the absurdity or destructiveness of the beliefs and values we live by or the promise that lies within them. In either case we are pushed beyond the boundaries of our present vision. Our percep- tions and language, our symbols and myths, are renewed or transformed. The area of what is real in our lives is extended through our encounter with the otherness of new worlds of possibility. The Roses describe it this way:

> Hope for the world lies in a shattering of old forms, in a reappropriation of life, first by recovering the freedom to act that is given with humanity, then by an exploratory life dedicated to the search for the fullness of time in time. The results must remain inconclusive. We have the possibility that the time of a new consciousness is at hand, the knowledge that, though the impulse may come from outside, the crucial response will be our own. Man's action makes a difference. And we know that it is perhaps this realization that makes possible the coming history that will . . . give birth to the new mythology.[23]

Robert Heinlein's novel *Stranger in a Strange Land* provides a good example of many of the elements of science fiction we have been discussing. The action of the novel takes place in the future, at a time when the planet Mars is being colonized. Life does exist on Mars, but Martians are quite a different species from humans; and, though little understood by earthlings, they are generally ignored as humans begin the establishment of a new earth on Mars. Although this is not a major point in the novel, it clearly reveals our inability to deal truly with the "other," the alien. We may travel to a new planet, but our human tendency toward conserving old forms leads us to ignore the new possibilities that may be present there. Instead, we simply duplicate the way of life we already know. However, Heinlein requires us (both the reader and certain earthlings in the novel) to take account of the "other" by presenting Valentine Michael Smith, born on Mars of parents from the first Earth expedition there but raised by Martians when all the other humans die. Thus, he is a human being, with all the potentialities—and only the potentialities—of a human being; but he takes on the culture of the Martians and develops human potentialities (such as telepathy and the ability to control his body—respiration and heart beat, e.g.—as well as the ability to leave his body) of which humans are generally unaware. When Smith is discovered and returned to Earth by a later expedition, earthlings once again reveal their inability to extend themselves through an encounter with something new by placing Smith in isolation and attempting to restore him to "normalcy."

[23]Rose and Rose, *The Shattered Ring*, pp. 121–22.

The novel is the story of Smith's initiation into humanity and the subsequent initiation of certain parts of humanity into Smith's world. He must first learn the English language. However, it soon becomes clear that the language barrier is a reality barrier. Smith cannot understand a word like "lie" because untruth has no reality to him. He also has difficulty understanding words and ideas associated with religion, because for him there is no reality to religion as one aspect of life. All of existence is sacred to him. He finally believes he has understood what humans mean by God and responds by saying to those around him—his "water brothers" with whom he has shared a glass of water (the source of life)— "thou art God." Life itself is sacred. But life can be lived wrongly; and if Smith "groks" (understands the deepest meaning of something) that a person or thing exists wrongly, he has the power to make it not be.

In *Stranger in a Strange Land* we are given the view of an "other," who is yet a human being, coming into our society, coming to understand or "grok" it, and responding by setting up a community—which he calls a church simply because this is the closest thing to earthlings' understanding of his way of life. The church communities or "nests" he sets up are to be the model for the future: people living together in love, harmony, and freedom. In this vision of possibility Heinlein carefully avoids the Edenic dream that childlike goodness is the hope of the future. Smith says that goodness is never enough. Goodness alone is destructive. Wisdom is also necessary, and wisdom (groking) comes with the proper teacher and a great deal of discipline. He further believes that wisdom, which gives power, will always result in moral action. If other humans share the understanding of the man from Mars, they, like him, will use their powers for "rightness." What is existing wrongly will be destroyed (discorporated), but this power will always be used for moral ends. Martians are contrasted with humans on this point. The wise "Old Ones" who rule Mars have the aesthetic as their chief concern. If they decide, as Smith feels they might, that the earth is not existing beautifully, they will destroy it. But for Smith and all other human beings, understanding leads not to aesthetic judgment but to moral judgment. We see in this understanding a view of human beings that begins in the garden of Eden: Adam and Eve eat of the tree of knowledge and become like God, knowing good and evil. Through Smith's knowledge, it will be possible for people really to understand the good; and, understanding it, they will do it.

This may well be an idealistic view of human beings. It is the understanding of the Christian tradition that knowledge and will are not enough. As Paul says, "I can will what is right, but I cannot do it" (Romans 7:18). It is not knowledge, but grace that saves. Heinlein's view is different from Christianity's in another way as well. It is understood by Smith and his followers that not all people will be able or willing to accept this new knowledge. There are evil people in the world who will continue to destroy unless they are destroyed. Thus, Smith discorporates any number of people (four hundred in one night) who are trying to capture him. This is moral because they are existing wrongly. Christianity is much more universal and egalitarian in its approach. All people are sinners and God's grace is equally available to all. The question Heinlein raises is, can we afford to be so accepting and egalitarian; or will those very qualities allow evil people to destroy our civilization? We may raise questions about Heinlein's vision, both in terms of its possibility and method. It does, however, present us with a view of the future in which wisdom and love and community sharing are a possibility; and in doing this it asks us to re-examine our own lives.

If such powers do lie within human potential, it is interesting to note that they can be understood—and so be realized—only by a transformation of our language. Every initiate must learn to speak Martian because English does not have the words to express Smith's wisdom. And without the words, we cannot have the concepts or the experience. We are thus invited to examine the limitations of our words and thoughts and to move to the boundaries of our perceptions that we might be open to new horizons of possibility.

At the end of the novel Smith offers himself to an angry mob and continues to preach his message—"Thou art God, I am God"—as the crowd stones him to death for blasphemy. The hero who brings the word of a new way of life must die, but his community lives on, and we are left with the possibility that human beings may yet discover their potentialities and move to a new age of love and community.

The Magic of Fantasy

Fantasy novels share with science fiction a sense of removal from the world we encounter every day, and they may serve the same function as science fiction as analyzed by Scholes. However, instead of creating a possible world that is made plausible by scientific and technological extension, fantasy mocks the plausible by asking us to believe in the magical. It is a prime characteristic of fantasy that it contradicts our normal and even reasonable expectations about what is possible. Science fiction writers sometimes boast that their fictional inventions of thirty years ago have become realities in the space age. This would never be true of fantasy, nor would a writer of fantasy wish it to be. The unexplainable and unpredictable are important to the world of fantasy. It is very often a part of the plot of a fantasy novel that, into a world already fantastic for the reader, an unknown and unexplainable power enters that causes the protagonist to cast aside his or her expectations about what is real. Tzvetan Todorov defines the fantastic as that moment when, for the characters, the "real" world begins to lose its predictability; and, though they try to deny it, they are finally forced to accept the incomprehensible, the magical.[24]

We see an excellent example of this in C. S. Lewis's *Till We Have Faces*, which is the retelling from a different perspective of the Greek myth of Psyche and Eros. The story is told by Orual, daughter of Trom, King of Glome, and is her complaint against — and final reconciliation with — the gods. As the story begins we find ourselves in a mysterious world and we know this is the region of fantasy. Central to the story is Orual's encounter with the mystery of the gods. Her tutor when she is young and her advisor when she becomes queen is a scholarly Greek who is nicknamed the Fox. Reason and clear-sightedness are of central importance to him. He sees the primitive worship of the goddess Ungit by the people of Glome as being dark, irrational superstition. The King agrees with the Fox about the darkness of the gods, but that does not take away their power:

> I, King, have dealt with the gods for three generations of men, and I know that they dazzle our eyes and flow in and out of one another like eddies on a river, and nothing that is said clearly can be said truly about them. Holy places are dark places. It is life and strength, not knowledge and words, that we get in them. Holy wisdom is not clear and thin like water, but thick and dark like blood.[25]

---

[24] See Tzvetan Todorov, *The Fantastic: A Structural Approach to a Literary Genre*, trans. Richard Howard (Cleveland: The Press of Case Western Reserve University, 1973), pp. 25–26.

[25] C. S. Lewis, *Till We Have Faces: A Myth Retold* (Grand Rapids: William B. Eerdmans Publishing Co., 1956), p. 50.

Orual is caught in between the teachings of the Fox and her father. She believes in the way of the Fox, the Greek way, yet the gods of her people still have a strong hold on her.

When her youngest sister Istra (whom the Fox calls Psyche) is offered to the Beast (who is also, in a mystery, the son of the goddess Ungit) to appease the gods and end the drought and famine in the land, Orual balances on the plane of mystery Todorov identifies as the fantastic. After Psyche has been left for the Beast, Orual goes to recover her remains and finds instead Psyche herself, apparently alive and very happy. She is the bride of the god and lives, she says, in a magnificent castle. Orual looks and sees nothing. Is Psyche mad? She must be, Orual thinks, for she cannot tolerate the possibility of the mystery of dark places. Even after she has a glimpse of the castle, she lets the Fox persuade her that such mysteries do not occur, that there are reasonable explanations for Psyche's actions and beliefs—perhaps madness—and that the dark, holy places do not exist at all.

The Fox stands for the enlightened man—that part of our heritage that comes largely from Greece. He is a very sympathetic character—kind, wise, concerned with truth and beauty. He is not simply a caricature of wrong-headed, blind thinking. Yet, as we and Orual come to see, he is wrong. She stands on that boundary, confronting within a fantasy realm for the reader, a realm of fantasy herself. And she moves, finally, in the only way possible within the world of the novel, toward belief, acceptance. Holy places may be dark places, but this is only because we cannot meet the gods face to face. Orual says at the end of her search, after visions reveal the truth of the mystery to her:

> I saw well why the gods do not speak to us openly, nor let us answer. Till that word can be dug out of us, why should they hear the babble that we think we mean? How can they meet us face to face till we have faces?[26]

To enter the realm of fantasy is to accept the incongruous, the irrational. It is to accept that the world is not all that it seems—and is more than it seems. There is mystery that, though it may appear dark, opens onto possibilities that promise wholeness and truth.

Fantasy persuades us to accept such a world, willingly to suspend our disbelief, not by creating a world whose surface looks much like our own and is readily believable, but through the power of the imagination, touching the depths of experiences that are part of all of us, at all times. Although fantasy is often concerned with specific social issues of a particular time, this

[26]Ibid., p. 294.

tendency toward universalizing emphasizes the importance in fantasy of myth and archetype. This subject will be explored further in chapter seven; but let us note here that we are dealing with that area of human life that is universal, though it takes the garb of particular forms, and timeless, though it appears and is apprehended only within the temporal. William Golding says, as he contrasts myth and fable, that fable is

> an invented thing on the surface whereas myth is something which comes out from the roots of things in the ancient sense of being the key to existence, the whole meaning of life, and experience as a whole.[27]

It is the roots we find in many fantasies, the roots to which still cling the ancient soil of primordial being. Thus, we encounter dragons and elves, unicorns and hobbits. Some of these fantastic creatures have an ancient tradition the writer calls upon (such as unicorns). Others are modern creations made to appear as ageless beings (such as hobbits). We may know unicorns and dragons do not exist; we may suspect they have never had being. However, we also know, as very real, the dangers—both external and internal—that dragons represent and call up in our being as we read of them, and we know the magic of unicorns insofar as the wonder of existence is a present reality to us. If these figures succeed in opening to us the unanalyzed reservoirs that come alive in our dreams and subtly influence our waking lives, we are in the presence of the archetypal. By externalizing and giving shape to these potentialities of existence, fantasy allows us to name them and make them our own: to slay the dragon and to wonder at the unicorn.

Of course the *story*—and so storytelling—is vital to fantasy. It is through the telling that we experience the dangers and delights of this mythic world. Most fantasies are strongly oriented around "plot" and are filled with adventure. This, coupled with their symbolic or mythic nature, leads many fantasies toward the allegorical. The danger is that there will be a "lesson" or idea the author has that is only thinly covered by rather lifeless and unreal characters. It will be the *idea* that is central. There is a message to be taught and it is presented in the guise of a fabulous adventure. We can say this character or event stands for this and remain on the ideational level without entering into a living world in the novel. We *think* about it without getting involved in the work of

[27]Quoted in Gunnar Urang, *Shadows of Heaven: Religion and Fantasy in the Writing of C. S. Lewis, Charles Williams and J. R. R. Tolkien* (Philadelphia: United Church Press, 1971), p. 140.

art itself. In the best fantasy this does not occur. The hypothetical, fabulous world must capture us on its own terms. We must become involved with the dragons or unicorns or hobbits in themselves—not simply in what they stand for.

J. R. R. Tolkien's work presents a good example of the creation of a world that is clearly not our own, yet in some unexpected way speaks very directly to who we are. In *Lord of the Rings* a rich and elaborate universe is created, which has its own geography, language, and inhabitants. The place is Middle-earth, the time is the Third Age; and we are swept into a world of hobbits (little people with hairy feet who seldom wear shoes and like to eat enormous amounts of food); Ents, such as Treebeard, who have both tree and human qualities and so serve to bridge the gap between human and nonhuman nature; and evil creatures such as the Balrog and Shelob. As Gunnar Urang points out, "to enter the 'other world' called Middle-earth is to encounter both the strange and the familiar and, emanating from them, an extraordinary power."[28] This power is closely related to the sense of wonder that is vital to all fantasy. There is a sense of the marvelous and magical that catches us by surprise and alters our way of seeing. Urang says, speaking of *Lord of the Rings:*

> What lifts this story, however, above mere "popular" fantasy fiction, what elicits a response beyond simple excitement and closer to authentic wonder is a certain tone and a certain aura of significance which are felt to surround the fantastic figures and their adventures. Northrop Frye and his disciples have taught us to account for much of this sense of import by identifying these figures as archetypal and the story as mythic. And it is clear that Tolkien does take much of his material from sources close to their roots in ritual and myth. We can detect archetypal resonance in certain images which take on a function reminiscent of motifs in primitive religions—the power emanating from the Ringwraiths, for example, or the healing touch of Aragorn the king, or the sense of the numinous about the wizard Gandalf:
>
> > "His hair was white as snow in the sunshine; and gleaming white was his robe; the eyes under his deep brows were bright, piercing as the rays of the sun; power was in his hand. Between wonder, joy, and fear they stood and found no words to say."[29]

Thus we find in fantasy both the story level with its allegorical concerns and the archetypal level, which is not to be thought about, but experienced. We see both of these operating as Tolkien

---

[28]Gunnar Urang, "Tolkien's Fantasy: The Phenomenology of Hope," *Shadows of Imagination: The Fantasies of C. S. Lewis, J. R. R. Tolkien, and Charles Williams,* ed. Mark R. Hillegas (Carbondale: Southern Illinois University Press, 1969), p. 97.

[29]Ibid., pp. 100–101.

draws us into the world of Middle-earth through the hobbit, Pippin, as he describes his experience of gazing into the eyes of Treebeard:

> One felt as if there was an enormous well behind them, filled up with ages of memory and long, slow, steady, thinking; but their surface was sparkling with the present: like sun shimmering on the outer leaves of a vast tree, or on the ripples of a very deep lake. I don't know, but it felt as if something that grew in the ground—asleep, you might say, or just feeling itself as something between root-tip and leaf-tip, between deep earth and sky had suddenly waked up, and was considering you with the same slow care that it had given to its own inside affairs for endless years.[30]

We enter into the experience of Pippin and a world in which Ents are a real presence, but we also move to a more thematic level as Treebeard helps us discover truths about the world we live in as he describes the way the evil force, Saruman, misuses the natural world:

> He is plotting to become a Power. He has a mind of metal and wheels; and he does not care for growing things, except as far as they serve him for the moment. . . . [Saruman] and his foul folk are making havoc now. Down on the borders they are felling trees—good trees. Some of the trees they just cut down and leave to rot. . . . Curse him, root and branch! Many of those trees were my friends, creatures I had known from nut and acorn; many had voices of their own that are lost for ever now. And there are wastes of stump and bramble where once there were singing groves.[31]

Through experiences such as these in Middle-earth we are made aware of how we have separated ourselves from the natural world and have desacralized it by our lack of awareness and care.

As a final example of fantasy and its link to possibility, we will look at Peter Beagle's *The Last Unicorn*. Beagle's novel is, as the title states, the story of the last unicorn. The unicorn leaves her enchanted, timeless forest to enter the temporal world of human beings in order to find and free the other unicorns who have been captured by the evil Red Bull. Of the many delightful aspects of this novel, we will look at only two: the entry into the secular world by the unicorn, which transforms the lives of those humans around her, and the transformations she goes through herself, from unicorn to human and back to unicorn.

---

[30]J. R. R. Tolkien, *The Lord of the Rings,* pt. 2: *The Two Towers* (Boston: Houghton Mifflin Co., 1966), pp. 66–67.
[31]Ibid., pp. 76–77.

Beagle causes his unicorn to move into the lives of people who have lost touch with the magic and wonder in life. This is best seen in Schmendrick the magician, who has lost his magical powers. However, on a broader level it is true of all the characters in the novel and, by extension, true of us. The unicorn, coming from a timeless realm, represents the transcendent, ultimate possibilities we have lost sight of and lost touch with in our secular everyday world. The unicorn restores the magician's powers, restores him to himself, we might say, and brings the reader into a world where wonder is found in the everyday. What seems impossible—the unicorn—opens new possibilities for what might actually be possible in our lives. This occurs for us because Beagle is able to make us believe in the world he has created. He teaches us to see with different eyes, to entertain new visions of reality.

As the novel begins and we move with the unicorn in her enchanted forest, we are charmed by the novelty of this fantasy. We know we are encountering a fabulous creature, and we delight in it—even as we withhold our total *belief* in this world. The proof that this holding back does not last is seen when the unicorn confronts the Red Bull and is about to be destroyed by him. Schmendrick, with the beginnings of the renewal of his powers of magic, transforms the unicorn into a beautiful young woman—whom the Red Bull has no interest in destroying. Thus she is saved from being captured but at the cost of becoming a human being. We as readers feel, with the unicorn and her friend Molly Grue, what a terrible thing this is—we have truly been captured by Beagle's magic and believe completely in the reality, the beauty, and the goodness of the unicorn. Having entered this new perspective and made it our world, we join the unicorn in questioning human existence. Because of the dishonesty and guile of humans she would rather be in any other mortal form. A rhinoceros, for instance, "is as ugly as a human being, and it too is going to die, but at least it never thinks that it is beautiful."[32] But the wise Schmendrick replies that a rhinoceros could never free the unicorns, nor care to. "Rhinoceri are not questing beasts," he says, "but young girls are" (p. 126). But, she complains, how can she exist in mortal form? "This body is dying. I can feel it rotting all around me. How can anything that is going to die be real? How can it be truly beautiful?" (p. 127). We feel the truth in the unicorn's question, but once again Schmendrick shows us the

---

[32]Peter Beagle, *The Last Unicorn* (New York: Ballantine Books, 1968), p. 126. The following quotations are taken from this edition.

other, human, view. He relates how he, a mortal human, was placed under a spell that made him immortal until his magical powers were restored. Thus, at this moment, he is himself beginning the change from the immortality he shared with the unicorn to the mortality of a human being. And he can say, though the unicorn (and perhaps the reader as well) cannot understand, "Whatever can die is beautiful—more beautiful than a unicorn, who lives forever, and who is the most beautiful creature in the world" (p. 128).

The three companions manage to get into the castle beneath which the Red Bull lives; and Schmendrick and Molly become part of the staff, as magician and cook. During this time the Lady Amalthea (as the unicorn is known in her human form) becomes real to us as a human person, and we witness her gradual acceptance of this role. Finally, gently, she falls in love with the King's son, Lir. When they at last confront the Red Bull again, Schmendrick is able to say the proper magic words that return the unicorn to her true form. At that moment, having regained his powers of magic—which come when he has regained his wholeness of self—he reenters the world of mortals. He begins, once again, to die—at the same moment, Lady Amalthea regains her immortality. As she hears the magician's incantation and knows what is happening, she utters a bitter cry and reaches out to the prince, her lover, whom she must now leave forever. Overcome by her despair, she has no will to fight the Red Bull; and he drives her mercilessly toward the sea, where he has enslaved all the other unicorns in the world. But Lir, willing to do anything for his beloved, places himself in the path of the Red Bull and is killed. The unicorn responds with rage and anguish— and drives the Red Bull into the sea, freeing the unicorns. But now, her task accomplished, her form and immortality restored, she can only leave the human, mortal world and return to her eternal forest. However, she is not the same as when she left. She knows what it is to be human, and she still experiences human emotions—regret and sadness—which no unicorn knows. She says, as she parts from Schmendrick,

> I will go back to my forest too, but I do not know if I will live contentedly there, or anywhere. I have been mortal, and some part of me is mortal yet. I am full of tears and hunger and the fear of death, though I cannot weep, and I want nothing, and I cannot die. I am not like the others now, for no unicorn was ever born who could regret, but I do. I regret. (P. 243—44)

We are also left at the end of the novel with a strange longing and regret. How beautiful is the unicorn! How enchanting and life-giving and tragic! We continue our story, as do Molly Grue and Schmendrick, a story that has an ending. But the story has been enriched as we have been touched by the enchanted, healing horn of the unicorn. We have seen new worlds of possibility and have glimpsed the joys and sorrows of humankind from a different perspective. Finally, our mortal lives have been touched by the presence of the eternal in the form of a unicorn, a symbol of wonder and possibility: and we can continue our story with a new awareness of the everyday world around us because we know that, though unseen, the unicorns are there.

The "magic presences" of which Gabriel Marcel speaks are alive among us. We are drawn into the world of possibility, of fantasy; and we are offered a glimpse of the "more" that transforms human existence. This is also true in science fiction and all other forms of literature. It is in the nature of works of the imagination to do just that. They present to us not what is, but what might be, and lure us toward new discoveries. By their structure they provide a vision of wholeness that awakens us to possibility in our lives. As we said earlier, the lure toward the More and the promise of wholeness are two characteristics of religious experience. This is not to say that literature becomes religion, but rather that literature in both its form and content (structure and themes) may help to open up those aspects of our lives that have been covered over in our secular world. Learning again to hear and see the magic that lies around us may help us to experience and respond to the More itself—the transcendent dimension of existence that grounds our lives and creates all possibilities.

Chapter Six
LITERATURE AS DIALOGUE

"To be is to be with" expresses a view of reality that asserts that life is lived in relation. It is through sharing with others — through dialogue—that our lives have meaning and wholeness. Dialogue means the sharing, communicating, and communing that occur between human beings, often through the use of language. We will discuss here the proposition that all literature is necessarily dialogical. Even though we generally do not speak directly to the person who wrote a novel, it is still necessary for us to respond—to answer the work of art—if we are to make it our own. Further, we will explore a view of reality that sees the decisive factor in all human existence as dialogue. Martin Buber's notion of "I and Thou" and Martin Heidegger's relational understanding of existence both include the assumption that "to be is to be with." Existence involves relation. This belief becomes the basis for their understanding of the religious dimension of life as well. We will concentrate on the dialogue that occurs through language and will investigate the developments that have occurred in our understanding and use of language in the twentieth century.

Storytelling, which is one aspect of dialogue, is, of course, essential to literature. It can also be seen as foundational for religious experience as the sacred stories or myths of a people provide the connection between their sacred and their secular lives. In the contemporary world we will see how storytelling has become a primary interest in any number of fields—religion and literature, as well as psychology, history, and philosophy. That we are so concerned with storytelling may indicate that we have lost the ability to tell our story, and it may indicate as well that we are searching for ways to tell our story because we realize this is a way of giving meaning and coherence to our lives. Can our experience of literature help us to recover this ability? Can it be a bridge to reconnect us with the sacred stories that integrate all aspects of our lives? Elie Wiesel says that "God made man because he loves stories."[1] If we lose the ability to tell the story of our lives, the story that creates a wholeness and coherence, it may be that we have lost our ability to stand in relation—in dialogue—with either our fellow human beings or the sacred.

A DIALOGICAL VIEW OF REALITY

In an essay in *Religion as Story*, Giles Gunn refers to Benjamin Demott's analysis of American culture in which he says we have very little awareness of others in our culture. We tend either to emphasize the ideal of the rugged individual, the self-made man, or to emphasize "an ego-transcending oneness of identity with other people," the obliteration of all individuality, the submersion in the community—the melting pot ideal, perhaps. In neither case is there an acceptance of the individual self in relation to another.[2] Thus, in neither case can dialogue occur.

We are locked into ourselves or lost to other selves if we cannot, through our imagination, entertain the possibility of otherness. The results are disastrous for both the individual and the community. Without the power of imaginative empathy we will not even tolerate, let alone appreciate, the differences between people that abound in our culture. On the individual level we will have consigned ourselves to a static identity that has no way of imagining what might be through the appropriation of alternative possibilities. On the religious level, there will be no way of conceiving of or apprehending the "Wholly Other" if we are unable to reach beyond ourselves.

The importance of recognizing otherness is illustrated by Charles Winquist's discussion of the necessity of contrast for consciousness. In *The Communion of Possibility* he says, "Consciousness occurs when there is sufficient contrast between what is and what can be—actual feelings and forms of possibility."[3] For example, to be conscious of a form or color, it must be set off *against* a ground. If the form and ground are the same color, the

---

[1]Elie Wiesel, epigraph, *The Gates of the Forest*, trans. Frances Frenaye (New York: Avon Books, 1967), p.10.

[2]Giles B. Gunn, "American Literature and the Imagination of Otherness," *Religion as Story*, ed. James B. Wiggins (New York: Harper & Row, 1975), p.65.

[3]Charles E. Winquist, *The Communion of Possibility* (Chico, Calif.: New Horizons Press, 1975), p.68.

form cannot be perceived. There may be hundreds of pink elephants on the pink wall, but they are imperceptible because there is no contrast.

Generally, when there is a contrast between figure and ground, we do not perceive the contrast, but rather the figure itself. However, there are occasions, on reflection, when the ground that makes consciousness of the form possible becomes the center of our attention as possibility; then we are struck by otherness. The possibility has been there all along, enabling consciousness; but the moment when we are aware of that possibility in itself, we encounter the other that has been present but unrecognized. This takes us beyond ourselves, and something new and before unimagined becomes possible for us as the otherness breaks in on our established reality. The relationship between figure and ground intrigues modern artists such as Escher, Magritte, and Dali (see fig. 6). Many of their works depend on the perspective change in which the ground becomes the figure. It has been there all along and is all the more striking because it has gone unnoticed. The relationship between figure and ground becomes central to our perception of the painting and we are struck by something new. It is only when the other is perceived as something other than the I that our consciousness may increase and our being in the world increase.

A dialogical view of reality begins with the affirmation of otherness and contrast. It must affirm as well that we are each finally individuals. Another person can never know just what it feels like to be me. Nor can I ever overcome the barriers that keep me from completely knowing another person. This allows for the otherness out of which new dimensions of experience can arise. This relates to our previous discussion of possibility (see chapter five), but we have here as well the added dimension of relatedness as the key to wholeness of existence and the necessity of perceiving the other as other for relation to occur. A dialogical view of reality, then, begins with the understanding that our being in the world is in relation. For Heidegger, to be is to be with.[4] Martin Buber says, "In the beginning is relation" and "All real living is meeting."[5] It is precisely the uniqueness and otherness of individuals that make dialogue possible. Only two separate beings can enter into relation.

---

[4]Martin Heidegger, *Being and Time,* trans. John Macquarrie and Edward Robinson (London: SCM Press, 1962), p.156–63.

[5]Martin Buber, *I and Thou,* 2nd ed., trans. Ronald Gregor Smith (New York: Charles Scribner's Sons, 1958), pp.27,11.

Figure 6. M.C. Escher, *Circle Limit IV* (Heaven and Hell), 1960. Woodcut.

Buber, in affirming the I-Thou meaning structure of the world, says, "Every real relation in the world rests on individuation, this is its joy—for only in this way is mutual knowledge of different beings won—and its limitation—for in this way perfect knowledge and being known are foregone."[6] The fullness of existence is in relation; yet our sharing with another requires that we be not one, but two, separate beings.

Language as the Mode of Relation

The way for human beings to be with one another is through language. Language conceived in its broadest sense includes all forms of human communication. All human creations are "words" because they show thought and they communicate. Tools or buildings, for example, reveal something of their culture and of the thought that conceived them. Works of art, of course, very obviously communicate—this is their intention, their reason for being. A sonata or a sculpture, then, can be called a word: it speaks, it creates communication between human beings. A literary work does the same; but, whereas the materials of a painting, for example—the oils and canvas—are not of themselves means of expression, the materials of a literary work are words. They can never stop speaking; they are always expressive. They can never be objects in the same way a painting can be. A novel or poem is only secondarily found in a place (a book)—words move in time; a poem is a voice that speaks more than it is an object. Words are not things, but cries.[7]

Walter Ong's analysis of human expression begins with this understanding of word and voice. He points out that the acts of speaking and hearing are dialectical processes. "The speaker listens while the hearer speaks."[8] As I speak to you there is an otherness inside me that listens to the words I say. At the same time, as you listen to me, you speak the words you hear to yourself and you respond to them. Gabriel Marcel says true communication is not comparable to "the passing of messages between a reception point and an emission point,"[9] or, as Ong puts it, communication is not

[6]Ibid., p.99.
[7]Walter Ong, S. J., "Voice as Summons for Belief: Literature, Faith, and the Divided Self," The Barbarian Within: And Other Fugitive Essays and Studies (New York: Macmillan Co., 1962), p.58.
[8]Ibid., p.1.
[9]Gabriel Marcel, The Mystery of Being, vol. 1: Reflection and Mystery, trans. G. S. Fraser (Chicago: Henry Regnery Co., 1960), p.252.

like a broadcasting station and a receiving set.[10] One party is not the active sender, the other the passive receiver. Speaker and listener must both speak and hear.

It is the possibility of hearing oneself and speaking as an other that makes human communication possible. Both sides of this dialectical process imply an otherness within the self, a split that both creates a tension within and makes it possible for us to communicate with another. This otherness means we can imagine what it is like to be another and so can "put ourselves in someone else's shoes." It also means we need others to come to a fuller understanding of ourselves. Being able to imagine what another person might feel or think is involved with the human capacity to take on a role. In the history of drama, actors have worn masks to indicate they were playing a role. The word applied to the mask, "persona" (that-through-which-the-sound-comes), is the source of our word "person."[11] To be human, Ong asserts, is to be able to take on a role, to imagine being other than what and who we are. It is also the ability to believe in the role of another, to be willing to suspend one's disbelief and enter into a work of the imagination. We are able to have the belief that there is a *person* whose voice we hear because we can imagine what it would be like to speak that voice ourselves.

This ability to believe in another is essential, Ong says, for communication to occur. Language in itself necessitates the belief in the other and the belief in the presence of an otherness in oneself.[12] He says it is not first of all a matter of believing that what a person says is true but rather believing *in* the person. This involves a trust and a commitment to an otherness that can become for us a presence. This belief enables us to speak, trusting that dialogue will occur. We must trust another person enough to let his or her voice become a real possibility for us; and we must be willing to hear that voice and, in that sense, to become the other person and open the dialectical process of speech in which being is shared. To believe in another is to look for a response from that person. When we speak, we must trust that our voice will be accepted, that someone will be willing to believe in us and listen and respond. We evoke a presence when we speak; we ask the other person to enter inside of us. We do this through voice, which comes from our interior self and enters another self; and, if

[10]Ong, "Voice as Summons for Belief," p.52.
[11]Ibid., p.54.
[12]Ibid., p.52.

the word is spoken from the presence within us and received by a presence without, two selves share in a reality of being—the I-Thou relationship of which Buber speaks—that is unavailable to either of the selves alone.

The second point—that we need others to come to an awareness of ourselves—further reinforces this dialogical understanding of human existence. Because we have an otherness within, as well as the ability to apprehend the otherness without, we require dialogue with another person to make that otherness our own and overcome the split within ourselves. We see examples of this presence of otherness as an individual discovers himself in Herman Hesse's *Demian* and Joseph Conrad's *The Secret Sharer*. The Secret Sharer in Conrad's short novel is a stowaway who has committed a crime—killed a man—on one ship and is taken in by the captain of another ship. The unnamed captain of the unnamed ship encounters the fugitive as the captain stands alone on his ship watching the darkness come over him. Out of the mysterious, dark and formless sea, the fugitive Leggatt emerges. This creates the sense of a dreamlike, subconscious world. The captain often doubts the reality of Leggatt, and perhaps we could say a new plane of reality is being explored. Leggatt often calls himself the captain's double, which further emphasizes the psychological nature of this encounter. There is a sense in which Leggatt represents that side of the loyal, upright captain that has not been explored—the otherness of the dark side within him, the dark side that would kill a man who disobeyed an order in the midst of a crisis. Through his encounter with this man the captain begins to experience himself. When he is above deck carrying out his duties, a part of him is clearly still below with Leggatt. When another captain comes on board seeking information about the fugitive, the captain claims to be hard of hearing so that Leggatt—his other self—might hear the conversation, too. The Secret Sharer must enter into his life for him to come to himself. In Conrad's story this sharing works both ways. Leggatt, also, clearly has something to gain through this sharing: he needs to hear the other captain's words so that he might know how best to find freedom. Thus, through this secret encounter the two men share a journey that leads to freedom. Leggatt leaves the ship as he came, disappearing into the darkness of the sea, setting out for the shore where he will be free. Through sharing in the life of one who has encountered the dark side, the captain has faced the limits and found a way to move beyond them. He is able to face himself more honestly and can accept the risks that one necessarily encounters when one acknowledges the otherness within.

A final point to Conrad's novel is the theme that dominates all his fiction. Each person is able to gain from this encounter because it is through sharing one's life with another that life is affirmed. "Human solidarity" is a key phrase for Conrad's work. He says, speaking of his understanding of art:

> [The artist] speaks to our capacity for delight and wonder, to the sense of mystery surrounding our lives; to our sense of pity, and beauty, and pain; to the latent feeling of fellowship with all creation—and to the subtle but invincible conviction of solidarity that knits together the loneliness of innumerable hearts, to the solidarity in dreams, in joy, in sorrow, in aspirations, in illusions, in hope, in fear, which binds men to each other, which binds together all humanity—the dead to the living and the living to the unborn.[13]

There is a great deal of darkness in Conrad's world, but through the encounter, through the experience of the solidarity of humankind, there is the experience of light and wholeness. The secret sharer allows us to face the otherness within and to know a new wholeness and freedom.

In Herman Hesse's novel *Demian* the emphasis is even more on the psychological dimensions of experience. The "other" is seen as a part of the self, a part that must be objectified in order to be encountered. The otherness within Emil Sinclair is objectified in the person of Demian. Although Demian is a person himself and has his own independent and, though mysterious, very significant existence, we feel this is at the same time an aspect of Sinclair's selfhood—the aspect that has been neglected and must be integrated if there is to be a wholeness in his life. As in Conrad's story, Demian in some ways represents the dark side: and, indeed, we do not doubt that Demian could break the laws of society if they interfered with his higher purposes. But he represents even more strongly the spiritual side of life, the side that extends beyond the dichotomies of divine and demonic and contains elements of each. We see Sinclair running from this person who seems to know him better than he knows himself. He turns to the lowest forms of degradation to deny this spiritual side, which is too fearsome. But finally he begins to discover Demian within himself. This occurs primarily through dreams and visions and through his art. Working out of dreams and his unconscious, he paints a picture that is a symbol, known to Demian, for the god Abraxas, the god who is beyond good and evil. And he paints a picture of a figure who is Demian, but is also Demian's mother (his anima in Jungian

---

[13]Joseph Conrad, "Preface," *The Nigger of the Narcissus* (New York: Dell Publishing Co., 1960), p.26.

terms) and is also himself. At the end of the novel when he has come back to Demian and to himself, he has a dream in which Demian says to him,

> Little Sinclair, listen: I will have to go away. Perhaps you'll need me again sometime. . . . . If you call me then I won't come crudely, on horseback or by train. You'll have to listen within yourself, then you will notice that I am within you.[14]

While Conrad's *The Secret Sharer* centers on human solidarity, Hesse's novel is more concerned with the individual quest. The narrator tells us at the beginning of *Demian*, "*We can understand one another; but each of us is able to interpret himself to himself alone.*"[15] But in both cases there is a clear sense that wholeness of being comes only through knowing the other who is oneself and encountering another outside oneself.

The Life of Dialogue in its Religious Dimensions

The understanding of existence we have seen—in terms of both literary analysis and life in the world—is based on an ultimate understanding of what being human means. This religious dimension is exemplified in Martin Buber's analysis of the I-Thou character of human existence. All life, he says, is lived in relation. "There is no *I* taken in itself, but only the *I* of the primary word *I-Thou* and the *I* of the primary word *I-It*."[16] The primary or basic words that are the foundations of existence are I-Thou and I-It. There is no "I" that stands alone. To exist means to be in the world, to be with the world. To be alive is to be related to other living things. Buber is speaking ontologically here. He is not saying what should be; he is describing what he believes is the foundational nature of what it means to be. But, as we see, there are two primary words: I-Thou and I-It. This is to say that we can relate to other beings either as subjects or as objects. We can either enter into a shared presence of life with them or we can use them for our own being without regard for their being. For Buber, wholeness of life is found only when, with one's whole being, one says "Thou" to another. When one says "It" and experiences the other as an object, it is never with one's whole being. "It" denies the ultimate dimension of being human in which one participates in

---

[14]Hermann Hesse, *Demian*, trans. Michael Roloff and Michael Lebeck (New York: Bantam Books, 1966), p.140.

[15]Ibid., p.4.

[16]Buber, *I and Thou*, p.4.

the sacred presence—God—which can never be object but is always subject. Thus, for Buber, the I-Thou of human relationships opens onto the religious dimension of life.

For Buber this wholeness of life is not found just through the sharing of relation between two human beings. One can have this I-Thou relation with any living thing. The spheres in which the world of relation arises are three: our life with nature, with other human beings, and with spiritual beings. In the first sphere the relation is below the level of human speech, but it is still possible to address and respond to another. For example, he says that one can consider a tree as an "It." One can measure it, identify it according to botanical classifications, or judge its usefulness for some human project; and in all these cases one never regards the tree as itself. But one can also enter into its presence as a Thou:

> It can, however, also come about, if I have both will and grace, that in considering the tree I become bound up in relation to it. The tree is now no longer *It*. I have been seized by the power of exclusiveness.[17]

This is not to give the tree a human consciousness but only to acknowledge it as a being and to affirm that being lives in relation to other being.

> The tree is no impression, no play of my imagination, no value depending on my mood; but it is bodied over against me and has to do with me, as I with it—only in a different way.
> Let no attempt be made to sap the strength from the meaning of the relation: relation is mutual. . . . I encounter no soul or dryad of the tree, but the tree itself.[18]

On the human level, relation occurs at the level of speech. To enter into relation with another person is, as with the tree, not to objectify, not to analyze appearance, not to judge actions. All these require a standing back, a separation of subject from object. Buber acknowledges that much of our life is, and must be, lived in the realm of I-It. We must treat other people as objects; only in this way can the everyday work of the world go on. But there are those special moments when that everydayness is transcended, when the true presence of the other is felt and shared. It is these moments that give meaning to the everydayness and sustain us through the experiences of I-It.

The third sphere of relation is with spiritual beings. Here, Buber says,

[17]Ibid., p.7.
[18]Ibid., p.8.

The relation is clouded, yet it discloses itself; it does not use speech, yet begets it. We perceive no *Thou*, but none the less we feel we are addressed and we answer—forming, thinking, acting. We speak the primary word with our being, though we cannot utter *Thou* with our lips.[19]

Thus, though beyond the level of human speech, it is the spiritual relation, the Eternal Thou (or God), that makes human speech and dialogue possible. Further, Buber says that this Eternal Thou is present in every I-Thou relation and, in fact, makes them possible.

In every sphere in its own way, through each process of becoming that is present to us we look out toward the fringe of the eternal *Thou*; in each we are aware of a breath from the eternal *Thou;* in each *Thou* we address the eternal *Thou*.[20]

The sacred is encountered within the sphere of relation. For Buber God is not to be sought through attempting to transcend the first two spheres of relation—the natural world and the human world—for it is in those very places the presence of the holy is felt. Nor is this presence to be found by an aggressive grasping; you grasp an object, destroying the possibility of an I-Thou relation. Gabriel Marcel differentiates Presence from an object by using the terms "inclining towards" and "gathering to oneself" or "welcoming" to describe the response to a presence and "grasping at" and "seizing" to describe the response to an object.[21] He emphasizes the mysterious nature of presence, which transcends all analysis.

A mystery is something in which I am myself involved, and it can therefore only be thought of as a sphere where the distinction between what is in me and what is before me loses its meaning and its initial validity.[22]

Buber uses the word "magic" to talk about this sense of mystery:

Believe in the simple magic of life, in service in the universe, and the meaning of that waiting, that alertness, that "craning of the neck" in creatures will dawn upon you. Every word would falsify; but look! round about you beings live their life, and to whatever point you turn you come upon being.[23]

---

[19]Ibid., p.6.
[20]Ibid.
[21]Marcel, *Mystery of Being,* p.255.
[22]Sam Keen, *Apology for Wonder* (New York: Harper & Row, 1969), p.25, quoting Gabriel Marcel, *Philosophy of Existence* (New York: Philosophical Library, 1949), p.2.
[23]Buber, *I and Thou,* p.15.

And finally,

> It is a finding without seeking, a discovering of the primal, of origin. His sense of *Thou*, which cannot be satiated till he finds the endless *Thou*, had the *Thou* present to it from the beginning; the presence had only to become wholly real to him in the reality of the hallowed life of the world.[24]

THE LANGUAGE OF DIALOGUE

Language has been an important concern in each aspect of this study, and we shall have to call on our previous discussions as we examine how it is that language is able to serve as a connecting bond between people and how this use of language is regarded in the contemporary world.

Our understanding of the power of language to bridge the gap between two separate individual beings and to create a dialogue, a sharing, between them must begin with the understanding of symbols discussed in chapter four. We looked at Kenneth Burke's description of language as dramatistic and scientistic: the first emphasizing language as act or word-event, the second emphasizing language as definition (used primarily to convey information). Ricoeur makes a complementary distinction between symbol and sign in talking about a symbol's "double intentionality" in which "the first, literal, obvious meaning itself points analogically to a second meaning which is not given otherwise than in it." Signs, on the other hand, are not opaque, as symbols, but are transparent because they "say only what they want to say in positing that which they signify." Because of this dual nature of signification, Ricoeur says, it is possible both to reduce language to characters, stripped of all but literal meaning, and to find a richness in it, "heavy with implicit intentionalities."[25]

In *The Burning Fountain: A Study in the Language of Symbolism,* Philip Wheelwright distinguishes between expressive language — the language of symbolism — and steno-language — the language of logical purity. He tells a story, taken from a legend in Estonia, to reveal his understanding of the possibilities of expressive language:

> The god of song Wannemunne once descended onto the Domberg, and there, in a sacred wood, played and sang music of divine beauty. All creatures were invited to listen, and they each learned some fragment of

---

[24]Ibid., p.80.
[25]See discussion of "Religious Symbols and Religious Language" in chapter 4 above.

wind caught and learned to re-echo the shrillest tones, and the birds the prelude of the song. The fishes stuck their heads as far as the eyes out of the water, but left their ears below the surface; they saw the movements of the god's mouth and imitated them, but remained dumb. Man alone grasped it all, and therefore his song pierces into the depths of the heart, and mounts upward to the dwellings of the gods.[26]

Expressive language, according to Wheelwright, is the language of the full song. It does more than record and transmit data from the empirical world; it communicates more than clear and distinct ideas that can be described without remainder and shared without ambiguity by all people. These are functions of steno-language and they are narrowly prescribed by the intention of this function of language. Steno-language, or literal language, is an essential part of our being in the world. It is necessary for many transactions that deal with the empirical world just because it *is* univocal—it speaks with one voice; and therefore it is able to serve as a vehicle for conveying information that can be understood, without ambiguity, by all who hear it. But this is not the language of the full song. Expressive language, the language of depth meanings, dwells within that area of human experience that is not available to logical or empirical verification. Not all our experiences are open to logical clarity, not all are without ambiguity. The language of the full song "pierces into the depths of the heart, and mounts upward to the dwellings of the gods"—the world that transcends our finite, empirical existence but also grounds it and gives meaning to it. This meaning cannot be expressed in univocal language, but this does not mean that this dimension of life is wholly subjective or nonpublic. It is possible to share, to communicate, this experience through multivalent, expressive language, language that does not categorize and limit but that expands our experience and allows us to share it with others. This language does not simply serve as a vehicle to transmit information, in which case the vehicle or words themselves could be left behind; but there is an organic relationship between the words and the experiences—the full song reaches into the depths of the heart and mounts up to the dwelling place of the gods. Therefore, the words cannot be left behind; only through them is the experience both known and shared.

Our discussion of steno-language recalls the positivistic stance of Hobbes and Comte described in chapter three. Steno-language to them would be the goal for all language, empirical verification

[26]Philip Wheelwright, *The Burning Fountain: A Study in the Language of Symbolism* (Bloomington: Indiana University Press, 1968), p.3.

being the key to determining what language "made sense" (referred to an observable fact) and what language was "non-sense." In the twentieth century this view was further elaborated by a movement in philosophy known as logical positivism. The early thought of Ludwig Wittgenstein was foundational in this movement; A. J. Ayer was one of his followers who continued this line of thought. The assumption behind the elevation of steno-language to the status of the only meaningful language is one that is common, to some degree, to all people living in the twentieth century. We have all been so influenced by the importance and power of scientific inquiry that it is second nature for us to look to methods of empirical verification when we meet with a phenomenon we do not understand. People often expect religion to provide the same kind of verification science does and may therefore attempt to prove the existence of God (as if God could be placed within a laboratory experiment) or to show how the creation story in Genesis is a more proper explanation than Darwin's theory of evolution (as if Genesis were attempting to give a scientific explanation of creation). If religion were trying to answer the same questions or give the same kind of answers as science it would seem that, as our scientific knowledge increased, the importance of religion would grow smaller and smaller.

It is to those who claim that religion gives the same kind of explanations as science that A. J. Ayer writes his *Language, Truth and Logic.* He spends a great deal of time demonstrating how aesthetic and religious statements cannot be empirically verified. On this point we would agree with him. In our terms, steno-language, which refers univocally to what it describes, is the language of empiricism. Religion and aesthetics, on the other hand, require the use of expressive language. He goes on to assert, however, that *only* steno-language is meaningful. Some statements of religion and art are propositions, but false; whereas others (such as any statement about God) are nonsense. Thus, by establishing certain rules for what will be meaningful statements (basically those that are empirically verifiable), he judges as meaningless or nonsense the language of ethics, aesthetics, and religion. Wheelwright comments on the phenomenon of semantic positivism:

> The semantic positivist starts off with a judgment about *language*. The only language that really means anything, he declares, is language which refers to things, events, and relations in the physical world. If it does not refer to the physical world, it does not refer to anything (for nothing else exists), and is therefore, strictly speaking, meaningless. By this bold stratagem the positivist gains an enviable advantage: instead of having to

argue with dissenters he need only declare that the terms in which they formulate their opposition do not conform to the conditions of meaningfulness which he has set up; in short, he dismisses them as talking nonsense.[27]

I. A. Richards is an example of a literary critic who attempts to conform to this way of analyzing language and to vindicate the imagination by showing that, although it does not perform a referential function, it does provide an important service through its emotive function. A referential function (to be *about something*) would require, according to this line of thought, empirical—scientific—verification. Since a poem is not "about" the world of sense, it must describe the emotive experience of the speaker. The example Wheelwright uses from Richards is John Clare's poetic description of the primrose:

> With its crimp and curdled leaf
> And its little brimming eye.

Is this a description of the object (a primrose) or of our experience while we are seeing the object? Richards makes a clear distinction between the "actual" primrose and our experience of sensing or imagining one. This experience is subjective and is not a description of the world but an expression of our feelings and attitudes. Thus, all poetry is emotive rather than referential. But, as Wheelwright points out, the distinction between object and experience is not so simple. It is "*the primrose as experienced.*"[28] Poetic language *is* emotive (experiential), but it is also referential. It is about something, in this case the primrose. "My thesis," Wheelwright says, "is that truly expressive symbolism . . . means, refers, awakens insight, *in and through* the emotions it engenders."[29] By making the referential and the emotive mutually exclusive by definition, Richards eliminates the possibility of talking meaningfully about this entire range of experience.

We may well ask how it is that Richards thinks by this approach to vindicate the imagination. By taking it out of what he sees to be a competition with science and logic, he hopes to show its value in another realm. This area is the emotional and attitudinal. Giving a behavioristic account of human existence, Richards likens the mind to a system of interests; and the goal of life is to achieve an equilibrium between these competing desires. It is not knowledge or truth (by which he means verifiable

[27]Ibid., pp.57–58.
[28]Ibid., p.60.
[29]Ibid., p.70.

statements) that can accomplish this (or at least not at the present time, he says). Knowledge cannot tell us what to feel. This is why poetry is of great importance. It shows us the balance or equilibrium we seek and helps us, by affecting our attitudes and emotions, to feel it.

The language of poetry that accomplishes this is made up of "pseudo-statements," that is, statements that cannot be verified. Therefore, they must not be believed in the same way scientific statements are. This was the mistake made at the time when what Richards calls the "Magical View" dominated human understanding. He defines that Magical View as "the belief in a world of spirits and powers which control events, and which can be evoked and, to some extent, controlled themselves by human practices."[30] This view has been largely overcome in the twentieth century, he says, though vestiges of it still haunt us and sometimes lead us to make wrong judgments about poetry. This mistaken view leads us to believe poetic (pseudo) statements are true and are about the world, rather than about our emotions and therefore nonreferential and subjective.

In this attempt to legitimize the imagination by establishing a role for it outside of the realm of truth and knowledge, Richards has destroyed the possibility of the "full song." Language cannot open for us the possibilities of existence that lie beyond the empirical and logical. Nor is it possible to share in dialogue as we have described it or to communicate meaningfully with another about anything outside the realm of science and logic. Wittgenstein says, at the end of one of his early works, *Tractatus Logico-Philosophicus,* "What we cannot speak about we must pass over in silence."[31] The song that could pierce to the depths of people's hearts and ascend to the place of the gods is mute.

Interestingly, many modern artists have, in fact, taken Wittgenstein's advice—though not for his reasons—and chosen silence as the appropriate voice for the artist. George Steiner, a contemporary literary critic, examines this idea in his book *Language and Silence.* He asserts that until the modern period,

the sphere of language encompassed nearly the whole of experience and reality; today, it comprises a narrower domain. . . . Large areas of meaning and praxis now belong to such non-verbal languages as mathematics, symbolic logic, and formulas of chemical or electronic relation. Other

---

[30]I. A. Richards, "Science and Poetry," *Poetries and Sciences* (New York: W. W. Norton and Co., 1970), p.51.

[31]Ludwig Wittgenstein, *Tractatus Logico-Philosophicus,* trans. D. F. Pears and B. F. McGuinness (London: Routledge and Kegan Paul, 1963), p.151.

areas belong to the sub-languages or anti-languages of non-objective art and *musique concrète*. The world of words has shrunk. One *cannot* talk of transfinite numbers except mathematically; one *should not*, suggests Wittgenstein, talk of ethics or aesthetics within the presently available categories of discourse. . . . The circle has narrowed tremendously, for was there anything under heaven, be it science, metaphysics, art, or music, of which a Shakespeare, a Donne, and a Milton could not speak naturally, to which their words did not have natural access?[32]

In addition to this development of special languages, which we do not all know and so cannot communicate in, language has lost its dominance on another ground as well. The power of the word, even when it is in a language we know, has diminished to a great degree. This is due partly to the emphasis on steno-language in our culture. But even more it is due to the overwhelming abundance of the word. Mass media bring the word to us in newspapers, television, and innumerable books. Advertisers manipulate the word to sell toothpaste through language that will speak persuasively to all people. Steiner points out that although the English language now contains about 600,000 words (compared to 150,000 at the time of Shakespeare), "fifty percent of modern colloquial speech in England and America comprises only thirty-four basic words."[33] If expressive, multivalent language is essential to the singing of the full song, is it any wonder that it no longer sings for us? When we limit our powers of speech we trap ourselves in very narrow confines, closing off the possibility of dialogue that opens to another person and to the sacred.

The response of the artist to these two phenomena, the emphasis on literal language and the loss of the power of the word through its misuse and overuse, has been to turn to silence. In the first case it is a silence that defies the ability of ordinary language to talk about art, to analyze, and to explain it. The felt danger is that language will trap the work of art (whether a painting or a poem) and reduce it to a category so that its uniqueness and life are lost. The artist at this point is quite in agreement with the view that says the language of art is not the language of science. And the artist would wish, as the positivist advises, that those who would attempt to understand the art work as univocal language would keep silent. What can one say about a painting by Jackson Pollock or a ready-made of Duchamp? When it comes to the arts of the word, however, it is more difficult to silence those who

[32]George Steiner, "The Retreat from the Word," *Language and Silence: Essays on Language, Literature, and the Inhuman* (New York: Atheneum, 1967), pp.24–25.
[33]Ibid., p.25.

would analyze. Insofar as words are used, conceptual meaning is inevitable. It is possible, though, to put words together in a way that we are unaccustomed to, thus requiring us to respond in new ways. If our old means of analysis and our usual categories will not work, perhaps our eyes will be opened to the unique reality of the work before us; and we will *experience* it rather than analyze it. Other writers have gone to the greater extreme of no longer writing at all.

If one of the intentions behind these tactics of silence has been to prevent the flattening out of a work of art by univocal analysis, an equally important goal has been the revitalization of language so that when people do hear a word it will have power. One way this is done is through the use of extraordinary language and structure in literary works. James Joyce's revitalization of English through the creation of a new vocabulary and the use of a variety of other languages is an example of this.[34] The poet Stéphane Mallarmé, writing in French, attempted to create a new language through giving new meanings to commonplace words so that we could not take them at face value as we might a television commercial, and dismiss them. This is a form of silence as the attempt is made to silence the old words so that words may again speak.

Another tactic has been the use of silence itself. Again, this has meant for some (such as Rimbaud) ceasing to write altogether. As a protest against the banalization of language (as well as its use for bestial ends, as in Nazi rhetoric), some poets have hoped to make the word be heard by no longer speaking. We hear so many words they become a baffle protecting us from the deepest experience, rather than leading us to the abode of the gods. Perhaps if we stop speaking we shall really have to listen. Steiner quotes from Kafka's parables: "Now the Sirens have a still more fatal weapon

---

[34]Here, for example, is the opening of James Joyce's *Finnegan's Wake:*

riverrun, past Eve and Adam's from swerve of shore to bend of bay, brings us by a commodius vicus of recirculation back to Howth Castle and Environs. . . .

The fall (bababadalgharaghtakamminarronnkonnbronntonnerronntuonnthunntrovarrhounawnskawntoohoohoordenenthurnuk!) of a once wallstrait old parr is retaled early in bed and later on life down through all christian minstrelsy. The great fall of the offwall entailed at such short notice the pftjschute of Finnegan, erse solid man, that the humptyhillhead of humself promptly sends an unquiring one well to the west in quest of his tumptytumtoes: and their upturnpikepointandplace is at the knock out in the park where oranges have been laid to rust upon the green since devlinsfirst loved livvy. (London: Faber and Faber, 1939), p.3.

than their song, namely their silence. And though admittedly such a thing has never happened, still it is conceivable that someone might possibly have escaped from their singing; but from their silence certainly never."[35] Steiner comments that, given the contemporary distrust of words, there will come a time when "there will be plays in which absolutely nothing is said, in which each personage will struggle to achieve the outrage or futility of speech only to have the sound turn to gibberish or die in their grimacing mouths. The first articulate word spoken will bring down the curtain."[36] In the art of the popular film we find Mel Brooks's 1976 *Silent Movie* in which only one word is spoken. Although words are written on the screen—as in the silent movies of the twenties and thirties—we do not hear the human voice—which as Ong says, has the power to open one person to another or the actors to the audience. The only word that is spoken is by the French mime Marcel Marceau (who in his profession never speaks), and the one word is "Non!"

In music we find John Cage using long periods of silence as part of his creations on the prepared piano. In the art film Andy Warhol uses both silence and lack of movement. His characters sit, silently, for inordinate periods of time. Our discomfort when we experience this phenomenon reveals that silence does indeed speak. We long for words to rush in to fill the space—empty, meaningless words will do. We are comfortable with them, no matter how sterile and lifeless they may be. So perhaps our artists are right to create for us silence.

However, we also know that if the language is to be revitalized, if the word is to speak again after the silence, we must rely on our artists. Those who turn their backs, finally, on the possibility of the full song accept defeat. We would hope to make a return to the roots of language, below the surface of empty words that dominate our speech, because only with the language of the full song is true dialogue possible. Language of the full song may open out on silence in the depths of our hearts and the abode of the gods, but much of the silence of our artists today speaks only of what we have lost.

---

[35]George Steiner, "Silence and the Poet," *Language and Silence*, p.54.
[36]Ibid., p. 52.

Silence and Dialogue in Modern Literature

The lack of communication is often found in modern literature, both as theme and as technique, to question the meaningfulness of existence. If human beings are essentially cut off from one another and no true dialogue is possible, what can one affirm in one's experience of the world? Yukio Mishima raises this question in his novel *The Temple of the Golden Pavilion* through his main character, Mizoguchi, who is literally cut off from communicating with other people by his inability to speak without stuttering. He sees himself as isolated from other people because of this deformity, which becomes a symbol for a spiritual deformity, an ugliness that is his whole existence. To him existence means destruction; his ugliness destroys the harmony that is his ideal. Reality for Mizoguchi is his stutter, his inability to communicate, the brokenness of being human. Dialogue is silenced, and shared existence is impossible. However, Mishima's novel presents a further comment on dialogue. On occasion, Mizoguchi does feel he is understood by another person. We may suspect that this is not in fact true, but his response to believing it is to feel blankness.[37] To be understood by another is to have one's individuality destroyed! Thus, there is safety in being cut off from others. It may be better to stutter and live destructively than to communicate and be destroyed by another.

Another threat to the security of Mizoguchi's isolated, destructive existence is the beauty of the Buddhist Temple where he is an acolyte. The boundaries between the religious and the aesthetic dissolve in the novel as this sacred, beautiful Temple becomes the bridge to the transcendent. The beauty of the Temple attracts Mizoguchi from the time he is a child. It is this beauty that leads him to join the Zen order so he can live in its presence. The Temple stands apart from the world of temporality, change, ugliness, and destruction that are his life. By entering into its serenity and stability, his own inadequate existence is made of no account. Mizoguchi, however, comes to hate this beauty. It pulls him away from his own life. Beauty insists on its own existence and in doing so denies his. Feeling betrayed by the one source of value he has experienced in his life, he determines to burn the Temple, to destroy the beauty, which is to destroy the only thing

[37]Yukio Mishima, *The Temple of the Golden Pavilion,* trans. Ivan Morris (New York: Berkeley Publishing Corp., 1971), p.270.

that has given meaning, however inadequate, to his life. Mizoguchi is left at the end, alive while the temple burns, feeling neither remorse nor pain. And we are left with emptiness. The life of isolation—the stuttering, disconnected existence—goes on. We have felt the weight of silence broken only by inarticulate speech.

In Franz Kafka's works the impossibility of communication dominates. If Joseph K. were to enter into relation with one person during the course of *The Trial*, we would have a sense of the possibility of meaning within the world Kafka has created. If the communication failed or was destroyed by forces beyond the control of the character, we would have a tragedy, but we would also have a meaningful universe in which tragedy was possible. However, everything in the novel seems to work against this possibility.

Joseph K. is awakened on the morning of his thirtieth birthday by two plain-clothes policemen who announce he is under arrest. They will tell him neither the charge nor on whose authority they are acting. For the next year, which is the entire course of the novel, Joseph K. attempts to discover what the charge against him is and how to fight it. The novel concludes the evening before his thirty-first birthday with his execution. There are two levels at which the lack of dialogue permeates the novel. The first is in terms of the court system that has (apparently) charged Joseph K. It is impossible for him (or for us) to know with certainty anything about the working of the court and its entangled bureaucracy. It would appear that this is an underground court system, with court rooms in various tenement buildings throughout the city, involving countless people so that at times it seems everyone works in some capacity for the court. This judicial system has, apparently, unlimited control over the lives of those it selects for judgment. All one can say about the court is "apparently" or "seemingly"; everything remains possibility for K. Whatever actuality there might be, K. has no way of knowing it. For example, when he first appears before the court, he notes that the magistrate is "fidgeting on his chair with embarrassment or impatience."[38] It is crucial for K. to know which—has he scored an important point in his defense, or is he simply boring or annoying the magistrate?—but K. does not know and neither do we. Together with the protagonist the reader is thrown into what Kafka understands the basic condition of humanity to be: each of

---

[38]Franz Kafka, *The Trial*, trans. Willa and Edwin Muir (New York: Random House, 1969), p.56.

us is imprisoned in a world of solitary isolation, cut off from an external reality we can know only by hints and guesses. Thus, no real communication can occur. K. cannot get his lawyer or any of those connected with the court to tell him what he is accused of. Thus, it is impossible for him to refute the charge.

In *The Trial* we have a character who is confronted by an ambiguous, *apparently* corrupt (for who can know for sure?) court system whose intention sometimes seems to be to ensure that no communication occurs. There is a barrier between K. and the court across which words cannot be spoken, and the outcome of this is his death. We do not, however, see K. as a hero wrongly cut off from the external world by an unjust court system. We think, in fact, that K. may indeed be guilty, just as the court asserts. He is a self-conscious, self-concerned person who is cut off from his associates at work and his friends much as he is cut off from the court. We see him sharing in real dialogue with no one. In his involvements with women we see no real caring or concern. In Buber's terms K. cannot experience another as "Thou" but only as "It." He is so concerned with himself and his *appearance* to others that he is unable to enter the reality of an I-Thou relationship.

Perhaps this is his crime. But even if it is (and we shall never know), we do not feel the (apparently) corrupt and irrational court has justified itself. We are left in a world of isolation and meaninglessness. It is as if the characters were moving their mouths, but no sound were heard. Each person is isolated in his or her own soundproof world. The novel reaches into the silence, but it is the silence of meaninglessness rather than that of the dwelling place of the gods.

In Samuel Beckett's *Waiting for Godot* we have not left the nightmarish world we discovered in Kafka's fiction, but we are now living a different nightmare. Rather than a crowded city filled with tenements and an overabundance of people, we find the two protagonists of Beckett's play, Vladimir and Estragon, alone in barren country with a single lifeless tree marking the landscape. They are encountered by two travelers and two messengers, but basically they have only each other. What they are doing at this place is waiting for Godot; and since Godot does not arrive, they continue to wait. They have conversations while they wait, conversations that are dragged out of the silence only with great effort. They usually speak in short phrases to each other, often only one word; and they seldom can remember what they said moments before. They usually talk about the simplest problems of their miserable existences—the boots and hats that do not fit, the carrots or turnips they have to eat—and about their most basic problem of waiting for Godot. They *think* he said he would come today and they *think* it was to this place he would come. But they are uncertain because of the difficulties of remembering; yet they cannot leave because perhaps they are right and perhaps he will come.

Dialogue does occur between these two men, dialogue that barely pulls itself out of the mire of chaos and speechlessness.

Estragon:	(violently). I'm hungry!
Vladimir:	Do you want a carrot?
Estragon:	Is that all there is?
Vladimir:	I might have some turnips.
Estragon:	Give me a carrot. . . . It's a turnip!
Vladimir:	Oh pardon! I could have sworn it was a carrot. . . . There, dear fellow. . . . Make it last, that's the end of them.
Estragon:	(chewing). I asked you a question.
Vladimir:	Ah.
Estragon:	Did you reply?
Vladimir:	How's the carrot?
Estragon:	It's a carrot.
Vladimir:	So much the better, so much the better. (Pause.) What was it you wanted to know?
Estragon:	I've forgotten. (Chews.) That's what annoys me. . . . I'll never forget this carrot. . . . Ah yes, now I remember.
Vladimir:	Well?
Estragon:	(his mouth full, vacuously). We're not tied?
Vladimir:	I don't hear a word you're saying.
Estragon:	(chews, swallows). I'm asking you if we're tied.
Vladimir:	Tied?
Estragon:	Ti-ed.
Vladimir:	How do you mean tied?
Estragon:	Down.
Vladimir:	But to whom? By whom?
Estragon:	To your man.
Vladimir:	To Godot? Tied to Godot! What an idea! No question of it. (Pause.) For the moment.
Estragon:	His name is Godot?
Vladimir:	I think so.
Estragon:	Fancy that.[39]

The great difficulty of conversing on the simplest level is seen, yet they persist throughout the play. Estragon says at one point, "In the meantime let us try and converse calmly, since we are

[39]Samuel Beckett, *Waiting for Godot* (New York: Grove Press, 1954), pp.13–14.

incapable of keeping silent."[40] He adds that they keep talking so they won't think. And indeed this does seem sometimes to be the case. They also keep talking to assure themselves that they exist. But this requires not only that each hears his own voice, but that the other person hears and speaks as well. Vladimir wakes Estragon from sleep, saying he is lonely and needs to speak to him.

The play ends with each of them muttering, "I can't go on," and the other denying it. And they do go on. They persist in waiting. And we feel quite certain that this is possible only because they do have each other. There is a caring revealed between the two men. Though the waiting may be meaningless, we sense a trace of meaning in their relationship. It is not much, but it may be all one can hope for in our world. The play is structured around the story of the crucifixion and resurrection. Vladimir speaks several times about the thieves who are crucified with Christ and the possibility that one of them was saved. The play itself takes place on Saturday (or at least they think it is Saturday), the day between the crucifixion and resurrection. It is a day of silence, or hopelessness, for the good news of the resurrection has not yet entered the world. Perhaps Beckett is suggesting that this is the world we live in, the world of Saturday. In such a world it is quite a triumph for our two bums, Vladimir and Estragon, to persevere at all. Their fragments of speech are a great victory in a world of emptiness and silence.

STORYTELLING AND THE RELIGIOUS DIMENSION OF EXISTENCE

We said earlier (see chapter five) that there is a wholeness, a completeness to stories that is not found in actual existence. In the three novels we have just looked at, novels in which silence or gibberish dominates, that wholeness is deliberately denied. Insofar as these are all works of art that have beginnings, middles, and ends, they cannot refute their own form. However, there is often an attempt in modern fiction to imitate what is believed to be the brokenness and meaninglessness of life. Obviously, if a novel were itself meaningless, we would have no desire to read it. However, the writer is able to use a coherent form to create an experience of incoherence.

[40]Ibid., p.40.

In Mishima's novel we feel the lack of resolution. The Temple is indeed destroyed, but the protagonist, choosing to sit on a hill smoking a cigarette while the Temple burns, leaves us with a discomforting feeling that nothing has been gained. He has lost the one thing that had occasionally given his life meaning and is now left with nothing. Kafka's novel leaves us with an even greater feeling of irresolution. Joseph K. is executed, which obviously is a definite, final action; but we still don't know why. "Like a dog," he says as the executioner's double-edged knife is thrust into his heart. But the statement too is double-edged. Is he condemning himself because he did not fight the court with more effectiveness? Or because he failed to acknowledge his guilt as the court requested? The novel itself is unfinished, according to Kafka. The beginning and ending of the manuscript are clear, but the intervening chapters were not left in any order by Kafka and one feels the arrangement is fairly arbitrary—which one does not expect in the novel form. In *Waiting for Godot* we feel we have come into the play in the middle; Vladimir and Estragon must have been going on like this for centuries! At the end of the play they are in much the same position as at the first. Perhaps tomorrow Godot will come. Vladimir sings a song at the beginning of the second act that mirrors the structure of the play:

> A dog came in the kitchen
> And stole a crust of bread.
> Then cook up with a ladle
> And beat him till he was dead.
>
> Then all the dogs came running
> And dug the dog a tomb
> And wrote upon the tombstone
> For the eyes of dogs to come:
>
> A dog came in the kitchen
> And stole a crust of bread. . . .[41]

The song is unending; the play is unending. There is always the waiting.

In these examples of modern literature we see revealed the pain of human consciousness and anxiety, alienation and loneliness, emptiness and the threat of meaninglessness. Dialogue is threatened; the story can hardly be told. The writers are not, of course, simply writing their individual stories. They believe that to some extent this is the story of our time—that we cannot tell our

---

[41]Ibid., p.37.

story or we have forgotten how or we do not have a story at all, which leaves us alone in a meaningless universe. Sam Keen has said that

> telling stories is functionally equivalent to belief in God, and, therefore, "the death of God" is best understood as modern man's inability to believe that human life is rendered ultimately meaningful by being incorporated into a story.[42]

Thus ours is a time when dialogue is threatened. It is also a time, however, when we have begun to talk about our story again. By calling the ability to tell any story into question perhaps modern storytellers have forced us to question our own story to see if we have one to tell.

Religion and Story

John Dunne begins his book *Time and Myth* by asking, "What kind of story are we in?"[43] The meaning of our lives takes on narrative form. We relate what we do and think and are in our lives by telling a story. We describe two events together, revealing the connection between them and the pattern of which they are a part, which are not apparent without the words that show their relationship. In order to see ourselves as selves and to see these selves in relation to others, we must be able to tell the story of the interrelationships of our experiences. Charles Winquist, in "The Act of Storytelling and the Self's Homecoming," describes the necessity of storytelling for self-understanding:

> The inability to tell a story leaves too large an unintelligible residue in our lives. There are too many feelings that lie fallow because we are not able to connect them with the reality of the self. The story can be viewed as an integrating structure that organizes our feelings and forms a sense of continuous identity. To live without a story is to be disconnected from our past and our future. Without a story we are bound to the immediacy of the moment and we are forever losing our grip on the reality of our own identity with the passage of discrete moments.[44]

A story takes place in time and so is able to take account of the unique moments of our past, present, and future. Yet because it is a story—an aesthetic form—it is able to give a pattern to the

---

[42]Sam Keen, *To A Dancing God* (New York: Harper and Row, 1970), p.86.

[43]John S. Dunne, *Time and Myth* (Garden City, N.Y.: Doubleday and Company, 1973), p.1.

[44]Charles E. Winquist, *Homecoming: Interpretation, Transformation and Individuation* (Chico, Ca.: Scholars Press, 1978), p.2.

passingness of time and so to create a connectedness and wholeness that are lacking in the simple passing of one moment after
another. As an aesthetic form a story is also important in providing
meaning and wholeness for life because of the role of possibility
discussed earlier. The story is able to gather up the fragments of
our moments because it is able to reach into the not-yet, future
possibilities that become available for actualization as they are
brought into our story. Both by hearing and telling a story we are
brought into the presence of something new, not yet realized, and
we are invited to become something more.

What story are *we* in? The fact that we can speak of "we,"
that we can imagine there is a story that is shared by more than
one person, reveals a double understanding of story. In terms of
self-understanding we have been speaking of individual stories.
Each person has her or his personal story—not totally isolated
from others, of course; there are no completely private stories. But
the story of my birth and growth, concerns and values, relates primarily to me. However, to have meaning that connects my story
to something beyond me, I must also share in a larger story, which
Dunne calls the story of my world.

> There is some profound link, it seems, between the story of a man's life
> and the story of his world. The story of his world is his myth, the story in
> which he lives, the greater story that encompasses the story of his life. To
> discover his myth he must go deeper into his life than he would if he
> were going to tell only his life story.[45]

To tell the story of the world and to see my story as a part of that
larger story is to give meaning to my story. Traditionally, it has
been the sacred stories of a people that have provided the story of
the world, the narrative of the way things really are, the drama of
a meaningful universe in which my life too has its part to play.
This is why Sam Keen says that telling stories is "functionally
equivalent" to belief in God. To tell the story of the world and to
see my life as a part of that story is to acknowledge that my story
is grounded in that which transcends me yet includes and transforms me. Dunne goes on to say that the story of the world is the
"human thing that mediates between man and the unknown."[46]
The story of the world is the human link to the sacred. For this
reason we might add that this story mediates between one person
and another and creates a community of persons who share
through dialogue the story of their world.

[45]Dunne, *Time and Myth*, p.50.
[46]Ibid., p.57.

As we look at Dunne's question a final time we see that he asks us, "What *kind* of story are we in?" He *assumes* that we are in a story, for only if we are can dialogue and growth and meaning be possibilities in our lives. It seems it is an impossibility for a person to be completely without a story and still be a conscious, living being with a past, present, and future. However, he asks, what *kind* of story? The kind of story we are in makes a difference to our lives. We could be living a story such as Kafka's Joseph K. in which the structure of the narrative form is barely discernable and the possibility of dialogue or growth or meaning scarcely present. Or we could be living the story of Vladimir and Estragon in which dialogue holds our world together, but so tentatively that we hover at the edge of meaninglessness. Or we could be living the story of Mizoguchi, cut off from life-sustaining relationships through our inability to communicate and driven to destroy all aesthetic forms that promise an order and wholeness that seem contradictory to our experience of life. Or we could be living the story of many positivists, which we might call the "story to end all stories."[47] This story would assert that we no longer need to live by narrative forms, that we have outgrown stories and can move from the particular and unique, which are characteristic of narratives, to the abstract and general, which can be verified by science and placed in a category. Thus, we must ask ourselves as we look at storytelling in our contemporary culture, do we have a story that we can tell about our lives and what kind of a story is it—a story of wholeness and promise or of alienation and brokenness? Do we have a story that is our link to the sacred?

The Possibility of Story in the Contemporary World

It is clear that for many people in our present culture the traditional sacred stories no longer provide the story of the world that transforms and gives meaning to the story of one's life. Even those to whom they do still speak may hear them in only part of their lives, while secularity and brokenness tell another story of their world. It is therefore not surprising that many of the stories we hear and tell in our contemporary culture are stories of brokenness, for those are the stories that tell of our experience of our world. But even to tell that story is, as Charles Winquist notes, to affirm the possibility of telling a story at all.[48] In that possibility

---

[47] James B. Wiggins, "Within and Without Stories," *Religion as Story,* p.3.
[48] Winquist, *Homecoming,* p.3–4.

we have an imaginative entrée into something more—the whole-ness and possibility implicit in the narrative form itself.

Thus, we must listen when our storytellers speak and we must continue to try to tell our story. The sacred stories of religious traditions are an obvious source we must not neglect. However, it may be that in our time it is also important to look to secular stories—the stories of our novelists and poets and dramatists. Through the experience of both dialogue and possibility we may learn again to tell and hear a story and in this way be brought back to sacred stories.

When we read a story, even though we are far from the teller, we are still participating in dialogue. The story is not self-con-tained. It does not exist in a book apart from a speaker and a hearer. Stories come from a consciousness and a context; and they occur, they take place, only as they are shared by another con-sciousness. Each time the story is told (and equally each time it is read—for we are still hearing the voice of the author through the masks of the work), we as hearers of the word are met by an otherness in whom we are willing to believe; and, in believing, we affirm the possibility of the interconnecting webs of life as well as the indissoluble uniqueness of the other and ourselves.

We are able to affirm the possibility of something other than what and who we are, with all the risk that entails; and we are able to affirm our dependence on the other to reveal to us who we are. Of course, the situation of storytelling in literature is different from the dialogue that takes place between two persons who are talking together. The author cannot hear our response as we enter into dialogue with the otherness of various personae we encounter in the work, but to write at all an author must be aware both of the otherness in him or herself and of the other who will hear and respond to the voice of the story. Both the reciting and the receiving of the story are ways of entering into the solidarity of human existence and the realm of possibility that have the power to transform us. Perhaps by listening to the storytellers of our time, whether they be telling sacred or secular stories, we will begin to hear and learn to tell the story of our lives and the story of our world.

It may be because we have lost the power of storytelling and have become aware of that loss in our lives that there is so much contemporary interest in storytelling. Although sacred stories are as old as human encounters with the sacred, contemporary theolo-gians of various persuasions are finding it useful to explore storytelling as a way of understanding and relating to the sacred.

Although with Judaism in particular to tell the story has always been an essential part of the tradition, Elie Wiesel has added a voice that is not only a part of his tradition but also a part of the unique circumstances of our culture, as he records Hasidic and Talmudic tales and tells his own stories. Within the discipline of clinical psychology it is obvious that telling one's story is central to therapy, but the contemporary emphasis in gestalt therapy involves a self-conscious effort to develop storytelling and role-playing as ways of coming to know the otherness in oneself and to accept the otherness of others. And, in the area of literature, although the structural device of a story within a story is by no means a new technique, the frequency with which it appears in contemporary fiction and the special use made of it again reveal the importance of storytelling and dialogue in our culture.

The phrase "a story within a story" refers to the technique in which a story frame is used to structure a novel. The novel using this structure usually begins at the end of the action and a narrator or the central character then proceeds to recount for us how that end was reached. By this device the author draws our attention to the fact that what we are hearing is a story. A narrator speaks to us, asks us to hear her or his story. We are invited to enter into dialogue. In novels written earlier in this century we see any number of artist-narrators or central characters who explore the possibility of creating a meaningful order within the world through the creation of a world of art—which generally is the novel we are reading. The "story" is obviously important in this, but it is story seen primarily as a work of art. What we see in a number of contemporary novels is an interest in story as a way of sharing life in order to discover a context in which life can be affirmed. The narrator-storyteller is still very often attempting to come to terms with his or her life and the telling of the story is a way of doing this, but now the emphasis is not on the work of art seen as separate from life so much as the power of human dialogue to provide a meaningful patterning of life.

We see an excellent example of this in Saul Bellow's *Herzog*. The novel is written in the third person and is the story of how Moses E. Herzog is able to move from a very neurotic period in his life in which he is unable to relate successfully to other people, to a point of transformation that permits him to accept himself and his world. The primary therapeutic tool in this process is the incessant letter-writing he carries on. He writes on scraps of paper to everyone from the President to God, Nietzsche to his psychiatrist. He never mails these letters, so essentially this is a dialogue with himself, as a preparation for dialogue with others. By being able to confront and encounter the other in his letters—and especially as he is able to confront the otherness in himself through projecting it out on the world—Herzog is able to accept the otherness that he cannot control, cannot impose himself on, cannot fully comprehend. He says, as he nears the end of his search,

> The dream of man's heart, however much we may distrust and resent it, is that life may complete itself in significant pattern. Some incomprehensible way. Before death. Not irrationally but incomprehensibly fulfilled.[49]

He comes to discover that incomprehensible pattern and fulfillment through the telling of his story. He senses a presence and his heart responds. "'Thou movest me.' That leaves no choice. Something produces intensity, a holy feeling, as oranges produce orange, as grass green, as birds heat" (p.414). At this point he can stop writing letters. His quest—for the moment—is complete. His story is told and so it now exists: a patterned, meaningful life. We discover that it is the character Herzog himself who is the narrator, who is writing about himself in the third person, when he says at one point, speaking directly to us, his hearers: "Thus I want you to see how I, Moses E. Herzog, am changing. I ask you to witness the miracle of his altered heart" (p.205). Through the telling of the story of his life he discovers the story of his world, which gives the story of his life meaning. Through the form of the novel we are invited to enter into the story of Moses E. Herzog; and perhaps through our witness to the miracle of his altered heart, we too will discover something about the story of our lives and our world.

Another example of the story within the story is found in Ralph Ellison's *Invisible Man* in which the nameless narrator, in a cellar in New York City, tells us his story of hope and disillusionment. At each stage of his experience as a black man in America his belief in people and ideas is viciously destroyed. This is the story he tells us. But he also tells us what he has learned while telling the story. He has seen a pattern of meaning emerge as it takes on the form of a story, and part of that meanng is sharing it with us. Through the dialogue he is able to see and appreciate an otherness that transcends the lack of meaning of the immediate events and reveals their larger meaning. In telling the story, which he thought would be a story of hate and despair, he discovers that

---

[49]Saul Bellow, *Herzog* (Greenwich, Conn: Fawcett Publications, 1961), p.370. The following quotations are taken from this edition.

although there is hate, he cannot stop loving; although there is chaos, there is also a meaningful pattern. Through this discovery he now knows he must leave his underground hole and enter again the world of otherness, the divided world of humanity. But not only has he come to a new understanding for himself by recounting his story; in the last line of the novel he says, "Who knows but that, on the lower frequencies, I speak for you?"[50]

As a final example we will look at Elie Wiesel's novel *The Oath*, which is made up of several layers of stories. The narrator is a young man who has despaired of life and is ready to commit suicide. He encounters, in Jerusalem, an old man named Azriel who swore an oath as a young man never to tell his story and the story of his community in Kolvillag. During the course of the novel the story is told; the young man takes it upon himself and is saved from suicide because he now has a story he must preserve. In much the way that Walter Ong describes how we take on the role of another in dialogue, the young man describes his experience as the story begins to unfold:

> There followed feverish days, filled with excitement. My involvement with Kolvillag became deeper, more intense, turned into obsession. I ate little, slept poorly. How can I explain its hold on me? I couldn't explain it to myself. Could I have seen in Azriel a personification of the prophet Elijah, the one the disinherited, the downtrodden dream about? Or of my grandfather, who died over there *in the tempest*? I couldn't say. Did he help me to escape? Accept myself? Fulfill myself? Possibly. It hardly matters. Psychoanalysis is not my strong point. Azriel knocked down the walls I had erected around myself. Something important and genuine happened to me while I discovered the city that lived inside him. By allowing me to enter his life, he gave meaning to mine. I lived on two levels, dwelt in two places, claimed more than one role as my own.[51]

We see a transformation occur in the young man as he enters Azriel's world and takes on his story. We also see something occur in the old man as he tells his story, the story he has sworn to keep hidden—and has for over fifty years. The story is not an unknown one in the Jewish community. It is, in fact, a most common story of irrational hatred and destruction being visited on the Jewish community. The occasion for this attack—or pogrom—on the Jews in Kolvillag is also a common one: a gentile boy, always a troublemaker and no one's favorite before, is missing; and the Christian townspeople, with a sudden concern for this trouble-maker, decide that the Jews must have killed him. There is no

---

[50]Ralph Ellison, *Invisible Man* (New York: Random House, 1972) p.439.
[51]Elie Wiesel, *The Oath* (New York: Avon Books, 1973); p.24.

reason in this. There is only growing mass hysteria and anger on the part of the Christians and fear on the part of the Jews that ends with a pogrom during which fires are started that destroy the entire city and all the people except young Azriel.

Azriel tells the young man this story only gradually and he says it is not his story so much as the story of Moshe, who is the town wise man and mad man (for perhaps to be wise in a world of pogroms and the holocaust is to be mad). When the outbreak of violence seems certain Moshe calls the Jews together in the synagogue and demands that they take an oath that, should any of them survive, the story of that destruction shall never be told. Part of the reason for this strange demand is related to our discussion of storytelling. To be able to tell the story of a pogrom or of the holocaust is to render it meaningful. This is what a story does. Therefore, to deny meaning to the event, silence is demanded. Another reason is the fear that the story may reveal possibilities that others had not thought of, and thus to tell the story may be to create the reality in yet another place. Again silence is the required response.

The strongest objection to this view comes from Azriel's father who is the scribe for the community: the one who tells and preserves the story by recording all the important events of the community. When Azriel's father sends him from the burning town the night of the pogrom, he gives the Book, the story of the community, to Azriel to take with him, even though he may never tell this story.

And so, many years later, when Azriel meets this young man, what compels him to break his oath and tell the story? It is a way of saving the young man's life; for once he has been entrusted with this story, he will have both a reason to go on living and a responsibility to do so. But Azriel realizes he is also doing it to save himself.

> Thank you, my boy. Thank you for disturbing me, shaking me. Thank you for crossing my path. I desperately needed you. Thank you for forcing my hand; you did it in time. Oh yes, I was living inside the closed world of memories. I liked my exile. I knew things by their names. I had lost my innocence, my need for worship that had been racking me for years. Worse, I no longer felt pain. A stranger to myself, a stranger to my own story, I was a poor participant in that of others. . . . That is why I shall speak to you in spite of everything. Out of gratitude. I shall break my oath not only to save you but also to save myself.[52]

In telling the story he comes to the understanding that it must be

[52]Ibid., p.97.

told—both the story and the silence. Both the storyteller and the hearer are transformed and perhaps those who hear (and we are the hearers as the young man tells us the story), those who enter this experience of disaster, will be bound—not by the oath never to tell the story, but by the oath never to allow the disaster to occur again.

We could recount any number of contemporary novels that share this story form. Whether they involve dialogue with the self, with the reader, or with another character, their shared commitment is that the story must be told. In the telling there is renewal of life. These life-giving stories may be our way of returning to our own stories, and through them to the story of our world, which is, at root, our sacred story. For now, this may be all we can do—tell the story; and, as a Hasidic tale records, this is sufficient: this brings us into the presence of the sacred, the dwelling place of the gods.

> When the great Israel Baal Shem Tov saw misfortune threatening the Jews, it was his custom to go into a certain part of the forest to meditate. There he would light a fire, say a special prayer, and the miracle would be accomplished and the misfortune averted.
>
> Later, when his disciple, the celebrated Maggid of Mezeritch, had occasion, for the same reason, to intercede with heaven, he would go to the same place in the forest and say: "Master of the Universe, listen! I do not know how to light the fire, but I am still able to say the prayer." And again the miracle would be accomplished.
>
> Still later, Moshe-Leib of Sassov, in order to save his people once more, would go into the forest and say: "I do not know the prayer, but I know the place and this must be sufficient." It was sufficient and the miracle was accomplished.
>
> Then it fell to Israel of Rizhin to overcome misfortune. Sitting in his armchair, his head in his hands, he spoke to God: "I am unable to light the fire and I do not know the prayer; I cannot even find the place in the forest. All I can do is tell the story, and this must be sufficient." And it was sufficient.[53]

[53]Elie Wiesel, *Souls on Fire: Portraits and Legends of Hasidic Masters,* trans. Marion Wiesel (New York: Random House, 1973), pp.167–68.

Chapter Seven
LITERATURE AS MYTHOPOESIS

The final angle of vision in our study of religion and literature suggests that through the imaginative mode universal patterns of human experience are revealed and, because we share in these archetypal patterns, meaning for our lives is confirmed. Storytelling is again important, but it is now the re-telling of mythic dreams that is central. Literature as mythopoesis transforms "the various mythological accounts into a single, unified work of art. Mytho-poesis, (from the Greek *poiein,* meaning to make, to create) *re*-creates the ancient stories."[1]

As we discussed in chapter two, traditionally myths or sacred stories were the bridge between beings and the source of being. They both provided the means of experiencing the sacred and gave expression to this experience. We have also discussed the way in which traditional myths have lost their power for many people in modern, secularized society. The stories that incorporate all aspects of life and give meaning to them seem to be unavailable to many modern people. Our lives reflect fragmentation rather than whole-ness, and we seem to be cut off from the source. T. S. Eliot's poem "The Waste Land" depicts the sterility and triviality of much of our existence. Eliot has many references to established mytholo-gies in his poem, but they are brought into our banal world where we have lost touch with the power of the other world except for the occasional glimpse of the side of it that inspires terror when we see the true dimensions of our separation from it and the conse-quent waste land of our lives. Many would agree that Eliot's poem, written in 1922, tells the story of the twentieth century. We live in a waste land and

---

[1]Harry Slochower, *Mythopoesis: Mythic Patterns in the Literary Classics* (Detroit: Wayne State University Press, 1970), p. 15.

. . . know only
A heap of broken images, where the sun beats,
And the dead tree gives no shelter, the cricket no relief,
And the dry stone no sound of water. (1.21–24)

The poem goes on, "Here is no water but only rock" (5.331). Water, the symbol found in countless mythologies as the giver of life and the bearer of spirit, is absent in this poem and, for the most part, in our world.

Martin Heidegger addresses this same understanding of the twentieth century in a different way. He says that we live in an in-between time, too late for the gods of the past (meaning that our access to the sacred is lost because our symbols and myths are no longer living) and too early for the new god. This is a time when the sacred is concealed from us. We have no language that calls us to Being, no stories we can tell that connect our lives with the source of life.

Before looking at the way modern theology and literature have sought to deal with this time of the waste land, we will look at the way symbolic language and myth functioned for pre-modern societies. We will also examine the relationship this has to Carl Jung's explorations of the archetypes of the collective unconscious.

THE MYTHIC CONSCIOUSNESS

Ernst Cassirer, in *Language and Myth*, identifies human beings as "symbol-making animals" and explores the way archaic people created and lived within a cosmos through the symbolic forms of myth and language. He concentrates on the process of myth-making and the structures of the mind that give mythic shape to the world, rather than on the content of the myths. He sees myth and language as the most basic symbolic forms, forms that con-stitute the totality of archaic people's world. He believes that neither language nor myth can be derived from the other but that they spring from a common root, and the beginnings of their development are closely interrelated. They are a way of ordering— they are the order—of the world for archaic people but in a way that is very different from the ordering power of modern analytical thought systems. Although language develops into a form that enables human beings to view their world theoretically (or to have a theoretical world), it begins in a way that is close to myth. The basic difference between theoretical and mythical thought is that with myth and the beginnings of language separate elements are not given. There is nothing to compare or analyze or relate to a more general idea; there is an undifferentiated whole from which separate ideas must be derived. The view of the world that results from this is synthetic rather than analytic. It is a dramatic world, governed by the law of metamorphosis, where feeling and immediate experience are the basic realities.

If, however, language and myth arise, in Cassirer's view, from an undifferentiated whole, how is it that they come into being at all? This happens when thought is "captivated and enthralled" by some object that confronts it in immediate experience. The whole person is focused on this point; she or he is "possessed" by it.

> When external reality is not merely viewed and contemplated, but overcomes a man in sheer immediacy, with emotions of fear or hope, terror or wish fulfillment: then the spark jumps somehow across, the tension finds release, as the subjective excitement becomes objectified, and confronts the mind as a god or a daemon.[2]

Thus, according to Cassirer, the primary function of linguistic concepts is not logical conceptualization, which brings together a large number of items under a common principle, but rather concentration on a single point. This concentration falls on those objects that are essential to the scheme of human experience; it is these that are first gathered from the flux of sense impressions, noticed, and named. As different items are subsumed under larger concepts, it again is not through a logical process of noting external similarities but because their function has the same or an analogous position in the order of human purposes and activities.

Since apprehension involves a great concentration of intensity at the point where the word emerges, the word is not a mere sign that points to an object: it is indissolubly merged with its object. This phenomenon seems to be part of both myth and language formation. To understand the analogous modes of evolution of these two forms, it is necessary to find their common point of beginning. Cassirer holds that no matter how widely the contents of myth and language may differ, the same form of mental conception occurs in both. It is the form one may denote as metaphorical thinking. In its narrow sense metaphor follows a process of taking two independent concepts that are in some sense analogous and then translating one into the other. This, as the logical process of conception, supposes that the individual concepts and a possible relationship between them is already given. What is required in myth and language conception is what Cassirer calls "radical metaphor." This requires the transformation, rather than translation, of a cognitive or emotive experience into a medium that is foreign to the experience—into sound. In this intense immediacy, there is a movement from the realm of the profane into the "holy."

In the dramatic confrontation of a person with external reality, a tension is released, giving expression to the feeling; and the word and the myth are objectified and so remain even after the feeling has passed. The word and the myth are both present in the initial utterance, the myth giving the sense of the holy and the word providing the material through which the myth can be expressed. This element of the holy accounts for the power that archaic people find in words. The name does not merely denote but actually is the essence of what it expresses. The potency of a thing is found in its name. We noted this view of the world in Jewish mysticism. God creates the world through speaking the word, so the word is the structure of the world. To know and experience the essence of something is to know and speak its name. This moment of numinosity is also a way of accounting for rituals. Both actions and words must be repeated exactly if the holy is to be recovered because the myth they reenact contains the essence of the holy.

When we turn to the area of psychology we see that Carl Jung's work, as Cassirer's, is basically concerned with human beings as symbol-makers and users. In his *Symbols of Transformation* Jung makes a distinction between what he calls directed thinking and fantasy thinking that is similar to Cassirer's distinction between theoretical and mythical thought. In our usual conscious thought processes we begin with an initial idea and without thinking back to it each time, but merely being guided by a sense of direction, we move forward through a series of separate, related ideas. This is reality thinking. It is directed outward and attempts to communicate. Fantasy thinking, on the other hand, moves without any conscious direction, apparently spontaneously and guided by unconscious motives. "The one produces innovations and adaptation, copies reality, and tries to act upon it; the other turns away from reality, sets free subjective tendencies, and, as regards adaptation, is unproductive."[3] Since productivity is such an important value to our "reality"- directed society, we should note that in Jung's scheme this is not to devalue fantasy thinking but rather to call our attention to new values: values of mythic consciousness.

---

[3] *The Collected Works of C. G. Jung,* vol. 5: *Symbols of Transformation,* eds., Herbert Read, Michael Fordham, Gerhard Adler, trans. R. F. C. Hull, 2nd ed. (Princeton: Princeton University Press, 1967), p. 18.

Jung contends that this symbolic expression of fantasy thinking is not merely a distortion of the objective world because the unconscious inner motive guiding these fantasy images can itself be seen to be an objective fact. He agrees with Cassirer that there is a definite relationship between this kind of thinking and that of archaic peoples. In our society we see these thought forms most clearly in children and in dream thinking. In these two areas we find a recapitulation of earlier evolutionary stages that are present in the collective unconscious.

In Jung's system the unconscious has two layers—the personal and the transpersonal or collective. The personal is composed of material that is unique to the individual and created out of her or his life. The collective unconscious, on the other hand, is "identical in all men and thus constitutes a common psychic substrate of a suprapersonal nature which is present in every one of us."[4] It is made up of the archetypes or dominants of the unconscious. Jung does not contend that the archetypes as such are inherited but rather that the possibility for their existence is inherited. That is, structurally the psyche possesses the "thought forms" that make possible the formation of archetypes. The archetypes are points of energy, potentialities that are themselves unrepresentable and become knowable to consciousness only as their effects are felt, enabling us to visualize them as archetypal images.

One theory Jung has for the origin of the archetypes postulates that they emerge from constantly repeated experiences of humanity.

> In so far as these images are more or less faithful replicas of psychic events, their archetypes, that is, their general characteristics which have been emphasized through the accumulation of similar experiences, also correspond to certain general characteristics of the physical world. Archetypal images can therefore be taken metaphorically, as intuitive concepts for physical phenomena.[5]

Jung cites the sun and moon as examples. These natural phenomena provide some of the most common and impressive experiences that appear to archaic people. Jung holds that although archaic people would not have much interest in giving causal, objective explanations for these phenomena, they would make every attempt to assimilate external experiences to their inner

---

[4]C. G. Jung, *Collected Works,* vol. 9: *The Archetypes and the Collective Unconscious* (Princeton: Princeton University Press, 1959), p. 4.

[5]C. G. Jung, *Two Essays on Analytical Psychology,* trans. R. F. C Hull (Cleveland: World Publishing Co., 1956), p. 105.

experience as psychic happenings. These mythologized processes of nature are not allegories of the objective but symbolic expressions of the inner that become accessible to consciousness through projection as they are mirrored in the events of nature.

Under the right conditions the archetypes, the dynamic nuclei of the unconscious, attract conscious ideas and become capable of conscious realization. The way they come to consciousness is through symbol and myth. They are first felt as an illumination (here we see that Cassirer's understanding of the formation of language and myth is quite similar) and when this feeling of the numinous is powerful enough, they are formulated as demonic or divine. According to Jung, "When an archetype appears . . . it always brings with it a certain influence or power by virtue of which it either exercises a numinous or a fascinating effect, or impels to action."[6] This could be either a moment of religious epiphany (or ecstacy) or the enactment of a ritual. This dynamic existence or effect, which is the heart of religion, according to Jung, is something that cannot be created by an act of the will.[7] By its very nature, it is impossible to create a living symbol. It is something that arises spontaneously out of the depths of the unconscious.

The symbol is the mediator between the conscious and the unconscious. This is its function: to bring the two together into harmonious, compensatory relationship and thus to achieve a wholeness of personality, which Jung calls individuation. This is to fulfill one's original, potential selfhood. The symbol is able to do this because of its ability to synthesize opposites. This is the symbol-forming function of the psyche, this urge toward reconciliation within the symbol. This is called its transcendent function; it is able to create a transition from one attitude to another. Since this is what the process of individuation involves, it is the symbol that is able to provide the bridge between the conscious and the unconscious and thus to bring about the reconciliation and wholeness. This is expressed in Jung's definition of an archetype: "An archetype . . . is a dynamic image, a fragment of the objective psyche, which can be truly understood only if experienced as a living opposite."[8]

---

[6]Ibid., p. 80.

[7]C. G. Jung, *Psychology and Religion* (New Haven: Yale University Press, 1963), p. 4.

[8]Jung, *Two Essays*, p. 120.

Of the many symbols Jung describes, two of the most important are the anima and the animus, the feminine element in the masculine psyche and the masculine element in the feminine psyche. "It is something that lives of itself, that makes us live; it is a life behind consciousness that cannot be completely integrated with it, but from which, on the contrary, consciousness arises."[9] Another archetypal image is that of the wise old man, which is an archetype of the spirit who symbolizes the preexistent meaning that lies amid the chaos of life. Other symbols may be abstract or geometrical, such as those that have always been used to denote wholeness and unity: the circle and the mandala (fig. 7).

Figure 7. Mandala.

Or the symbol may take the human form of the hero, which is a symbol of the libido.

> Here the symbolism leaves the objective, material realm of astral and meterological images and takes on human form, changing into a figure who passes from joy to sorrow, from sorrow to joy, and, like the sun, now stands high at the zenith and now is plunged into darkest night, only to rise again in new splendour. Just as the sun . . . , man sets his course by immutable laws and, his journey over, sinks into darkness, to rise again in his children and begin the cycle anew.[10]

The power behind these archetypes, "mana," is a primordial idea of energy that is found in the most widely separated archaic

[9]Jung, *Collected Works,* 9:27.
[10]Jung, *Collected Works,* 5:171.

religions. This power concept, as both Jung and Cassirer point out, is the earliest form of a concept of God among archaic people. It is mana in its positive form, taboo in its negative—both of these are beyond the realm of the profane and are the energy that is transmitted through the archetypal images and is experienced as the numinous.

It is within this experience of the numinous that human beings feel their person threatened:

> The collective unconscious is anything but an incapsulated personal system; it is sheer objectivity, as wide as the world and open to all the world. There I am the object of every subject, in complete reversal of my ordinary consciousness, where I am always the subject that has an object. There I am utterly one with the world, so much a part of it that I forget all too easily who I really am. . . . That is the age-old danger, instinctively known and feared by primitive man, who himself stands so very close to [unconsciousness].[11]

This sense of undifferentiated power is what human beings, in their efforts at civilization, attempt to come to terms with. Symbols and myths, in bringing consciousness into participation with this power in the transcendent function, are able to achieve this. The forms of ritual and dogma that are a part of every culture are even more conscious ways of dealing with this danger. They provide safety by taking away the power of the immediacy of the experience by containing it within certain formulae. It is possible for the transcendent function still to be served through these means, but there is also the danger that the forms will become so rigid and consciously devised and understood that they no longer are vehicles for the experience of numinosity but cut off all possibility of such an experience. It is such a thing, perhaps, that has happened in our time. It is not that the numinous is not all around us, as it was around archaic people: it cannot be lessened by our emphasis on reason and consciousness. But just because of this emphasis, the numinous is not often experienced in our era; we have found no suitable symbols through which we can accept this experience. As Jung says, in giving an apologetic for his work: only an unparalleled impoverishment of symbolism could enable us to rediscover the gods as psychic factors—as archetypes of the unconscious. All our talk of the unconscious would be superfluous in an age that possessed symbols.[12]

---

[11]Jung, *Collected Works,* 9:22.
[12]Ibid., p. 23.

Archetypal Literary Criticism

Northrop Frye is a literary critic to whom the concepts of archetype and myth are very important. His intention in his work *Anatomy of Criticism* is to establish a structure for including and understanding all forms of literature. His assumption is that there is an order of words similar to the order of nature and thus it is possible to discover and give systematic expression to this order. Mythology is of central importance to Frye in this discovery.

> Mythology as a total structure, defining as it does a society's religious beliefs, historical traditions, cosmological speculations—in short, the whole range of its verbal expressiveness—is the matrix of literature, and major poetry keeps returning to it.[13]

Myth, providing a total universe as it does, gives the outlines for our whole verbal universe; and literature, as it develops, merges into and with myth.

Frye attempts to establish the relationship between myth and literature through the study of genres and conventions of literature. Recurrent imagery is one of the aspects of this study. When we examine literature in a wide variety of times and places we see that certain images, themes, and symbols repeat themselves. This recurrence indicates to Frye a certain unity in the nature that is imitated by literature as well as in the forms that literature takes. He terms these recurring images "archetypes," and defines an archetype as "a symbol which connects one poem with another and thereby helps to unify and integrate our literary experience."[14] One senses in these repeated images some sort of pattern or model behind their creation. They thus can be seen not only as a way of giving literary criticism a way of talking about literature but also as structural principles of the literary form itself. They structure our expression and experience of literature just as, in the psychological realm, archetypes in Jung's understanding structure our psychic experience of the world. Frye observes that these archetypes reappear in the greatest works of literature; in fact, a classic is one that enables us to see large numbers of converging patterns of significance. We can see literature, then, as having a mythical shape that leads us finally to some unseen center of the order of words where we find universal symbols.

---

[13]Northrop Frye, *Fables of Identity: Studies in Poetic Mythology* (New York: Harcourt, Brace & World, 1963), p. 33.

[14]Northrop Frye, *Anatomy of Criticism* (New York: Atheneum, 1965), p. 18.

Frye sees this recurrence not only in the imagery of a work of art but also in its very structure. A work of art presents itself both in time and in space. The temporal element is the rhythm, the spatial is the pattern. The rhythm is the narrative—the linear movement of the work. The pattern is the meaning or significance of the work—the integrity of form. Adapting Aristotle's terms, he calls these elements *dianoia* and *mythos*. Frye uses the term *narrative* to describe the continuous recognition of credibility that one feels while experiencing a work of art and *pattern* to describe the recognition of the identity of the total design that one possesses after the immediate experience of the work is over. With this latter experience, every event becomes a manifestation of an underlying unity within the work, a unity that involves both *mythos* and *dianoia*. *Mythos* is *dianoia* in movement; *dianoia* is *mythos* in stasis.

These terms take on further meaning as we see them in the context of mythical thinking. The origin of narrative lies in ritual, understood as the temporal sequence of acts in which conscious meaning is latent. Ritual tends toward pure narrative, which would be automatic, unconscious repetition. Patterns of imagery are oracular in origin. They are filled with instantaneous comprehension with no reference to time. Pure pattern would end in an incommunicable state of consciousness.

Frye asserts that this recurrence in both art and ritual is founded on the natural cycle, and in this sense art imitates nature as a cyclical process. The cyclical movements of the sun, moon, seasons, and human life become the foci around which symbols organize themselves. Frye sees human experience, as it is reflected in both literature and ritual, as falling into four main mythical movements, corresponding to the four seasons (spring, summer, fall, winter), the four periods of the day (morning, noon, evening, night), the four stages of life (youth, maturity, age, death), etc. The four literary categories, or mythoi, paralleling these are the comic, the romantic, the tragic, and the ironic (fig. 8).

Any work of literature would fall into one of these categories and would share certain characteristics in common with all other works in that category. Frye assumes that there are certain colors, certain types of characters and relationships they would have, certain landscapes or settings, certain structures of development and endings—and on and on—that will cluster around each of the seasons and mythoi. By discovering these elements in a work of literature one is able to see how the particular work fits into a larger, universal pattern. This gives us a sense of recognition of the archetypes that are foundational in our own experience.

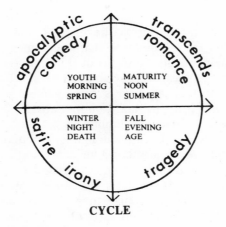

Figure 8. Frye's Mythoi, described in *Anatomy of Criticism*.

Let us look, for example, at the mythos of summer, romance. The essential plot of romance is adventure, and the central adventure that gives form to romance is the quest. Frye sees four stages within the quest theme: the *agon* or conflict of the perilous journey, the pathos or death struggle, the disappearance of the hero, and his reappearance and recognition. These four stages are parallel to the four mythoi themselves: romance, tragedy, irony, and comedy; and thus the mythoi can be seen as parts of one unified myth.

It is interesting to compare Joseph Campbell's work on myth and hero in which he envisions a "monomyth" that, with minor variations, can be found in all cultures at all times. His concern is with the myths around which peoples have organized their lives, rather than with literature; but with Frye he discovers patterns of universal significance all human beings share in. In his work *Hero With a Thousand Faces* he examines the stories that cultures have told about their heroes in fairy tales, myths, and legends under the triadic structure of the separation or departure of the hero, the trials and victories of initiation, and the return and reintegration with society. Although Campbell uses three rather than the four basic elements Frye does, one can trace the same steps in each. The quest of the hero centers, as Campbell describes it, around the fact that:

He and/or the world in which he finds himself suffers from a symbolical deficiency. In fairy tales this may be as slight as the lack of a certain golden ring, whereas in apocalyptic vision the physical and spiritual life of the whole earth can be represented as fallen, or on the point of falling, into ruin.[15]

Frye says that in dream terms the quest romance is seen as a search of the self for a fulfillment that overcomes the anxieties of reality, yet contains reality. In terms of ritual, it is seen as a victory of fertility over the waste land. Campbell says, "The effect of the successful adventure of the hero is the unlocking and release again of the flow of life into the body of the world."[16] For both, the quest is completed when the emptiness is filled, when the lost treasure, without which life is meaningless, is found (fig. 9).

These themes, which are found in sacred and secular stories of all people, as well as in their art and dreams, are seen by this view to be the way human existence is structured. These stories about heroes are familiar to us because they are our stories. We must have access to these structured accounts of reality which are not fictions but the stories of our lives, if we are to live in the presence of our total selves and the source of our being. Campbell shares this understanding of the role of myth:

Throughout the inhabited world, in all times and under every circumstance, the myths of man have flourished; and they have been the living inspiration of whatever else may have appeared out of the activities of the human body and mind. It would not be too much to say that myth is the secret opening through which the inexhaustible energies of the cosmos pour into human cultural manifestation. Religions, philosophies, arts, the social forms of primitive and historic man, prime discoveries in science and technology, the very dreams that blister sleep, boil up from the basic, magic ring of myth. . . . In the absence of an effective general mythology, each of us has his private, unrecognized, rudimentary, yet secretly potent pantheon of dream.[17]

Frye believes that literature, when it is seen in its most far-reaching dimensions, imitates the total dream of human beings, total possibility that is not in the center of reality, but at its circumference. Nature is no longer the container of the literary universe but is the thing contained. The understanding of literature Frye envisions is "a world of total metaphor, in which everything is

---

[15]Joseph Campbell, *The Hero with a Thousand Faces,* Bollingen Series 17 (Princeton: Princeton University Press, 1972), p. 37.
[16]Ibid., p. 40.
[17]Ibid., pp. 3–4.

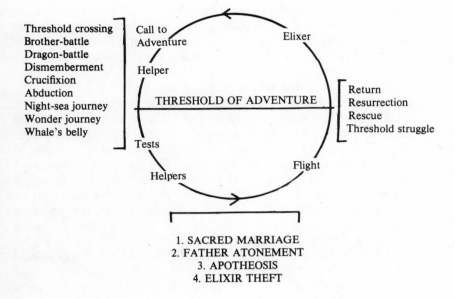

Threshold crossing
Brother-battle
Dragon-battle
Dismemberment
Crucifixion
Abduction
Night-sea journey
Wonder journey
Whale's belly

Call to Adventure

Elixer

Helper

THRESHOLD OF ADVENTURE

Return
Resurrection
Rescue
Threshold struggle

Tests

Helpers

Flight

1. SACRED MARRIAGE
2. FATHER ATONEMENT
3. APOTHEOSIS
4. ELIXIR THEFT

The mythological hero, setting forth from his commonday hut or castle, is lured, carried away, or else voluntarily proceeds, to the threshold of adventure. There he encounters a shadow presence that guards the passage. The hero may defeat or conciliate this power and go alive into the kingdom of the dark (brother-battle, dragon-battle; offering, charm), or be slain by the opponent and descend in death (dismemberment, crucifixion). Beyond the threshold, then, the hero journeys through a world of unfamiliar yet strangely intimate forces, some of which severely threaten him (tests), some of which give magical aid (helpers). When he arrives at the nadir of the mythological round, he undergoes a supreme ordeal and gains his reward. The triumph may be represented as the hero's sexual union with the goddess-mother of the world (sacred marriage), his recognition by the father-creator (father atonement), his own divinization (apotheosis), or again— if the powers have remained unfriendly to him— his theft of the boon he came to gain (bride-theft, fire-theft); intrinsically it is an expansion of consciousness and therewith of being (illumination, transfiguration, freedom). The final work is that of the return. If the powers have blessed the hero, he now sets forth under their protection (emissary); if not, he flees and is pursued (transformation flight, obstacle flight). At the return threshold the transcendental powers must remain behind; the hero re-emerges from the kingdom of dread (return, resurrection). The boon that he brings restores the world (elixir).

Figure 9. Joseph Campbell's Monomyth, *The Hero with a Thousand Faces*, Bollingen Series 17, (Princeton: Princeton University Press, 1972), pp. 245-46.

potentially identical with everything else."[18] Poetry unites total ritual, or unlimited social action, with total dream, or unlimited individual thought. Literature is no longer a commentary on life or reality when understood in this way but contains life and reality in a system of verbal relationships.

Frye specifies that this is not to make literature into religion: each must maintain its own integrity, but the function he describes for literature certainly parallels that of religion. The poetic symbol has the power to bring together event and idea, example and precept, ritual and dream, action and thought. The power that is created when these elements come together generates a wholeness and integrity reminiscent of Cassirer's radical metaphor in which the word comes into being within the realm of the holy and of Jung's symbols of transformation that also bring two areas together and produce wholeness of being. So, too, for Frye the formation occurs outside the realm of the profane; he uses Eliade's phrase, *in illo tempore,* to describe it.[19] Frye refers to Søren Kierkegaard's work *Repetition* to describe what is involved in the mysterious transforming power of a work of art. Kierkegaard uses the term "repetition" to mean "not the simple repeating of an experience, but the recreating of it which redeems or awakens it to life, the end of the process, he says, being the apocalyptic promise: 'Behold, I make all things new.'"[20] The literary universe is enlarged to the point that it seems strangely like the universe we live in—our total field of knowing, experiencing, feeling, living. With such a view, our attempt to understand literature, which is the function of literary criticism, will lead to "reforging the broken links between creation and knowledge, art and science, myth and concept."[21] The act of re-creation becomes possible through our understanding the total, mythic structure of literature that contains the structural possibilities of our existence.

Myth and Archetype in Modern Literature

The interest in myth and archetype we have seen in the fields of psychology, philosophy, comparative religions, and literary criticism is also found among creative artists in the twentieth century.

---

[18]Frye, *Anatomy of Criticism,* p. 136.
[19]Frye, *Fabels of Identity,* p. 30.
[20]Frye, *Anatomy of Criticism,* p. 345.
[21]Ibid., p. 354.

We will point to just a few examples of the way poets and novelists have deliberately incorporated established mythic structures into their works. Of course, the theories we have been discussing indicate that *any* work of art could be examined by archetypal criticism. A writer cannot avoid using mythic structures if they are the given building blocks of our expression and experience. But artists have deliberately chosen mythopoesis by turning to established mythologies to give shape to contemporary experience. Two of the most significant literary works of the twentieth century, James Joyce's novel *Ulysses* and T. S. Eliot's poem "The Waste Land" make extensive use of mythology. Eliot makes the following statement about Joyce's work, and it could be applied to the use of myth by many modern artists:

> In using the myth, in manipulating a continuous parallel between contemporaneity and antiquity, Mr. Joyce is pursuing a method which others must pursue after him. . . . It is simply a way of controlling, of ordering, of giving a shape and a significance to the immense panorama of futility and anarchy which is contemporary history. . . . Instead of narrative method, we may now use the mythical method. It is, I seriously believe, a step toward making the modern world possible for art.[22]

Why is there any question about the possibility of art in the modern world? Art, as part of the total cultural matrix of a period, necessarily grows out of the resources of the age. It both reflects and molds the consciousness of its time, but it cannot be inconsistent with it. The art of our culture must therefore reflect the fragmentation and broken center—the lack of a consistent mythology that patterns the experiences of a culture. And since a work of art *must* pattern experience, must create a wholeness if it is to be a work of art, how can the artist work in the modern period and be true both to his or her culture and to the medium of art? It is in answer to this question that Eliot suggests the artist can use mythologies that were consciously acknowledged as the stories of earlier times; and by running them parallel with contemporary experience the poet can reveal both the fragmentation and the blunted, but still real, connections that exist with persistent archetypal patterns. As Jung said that our talk about the unconscious would be superfluous in an age that possessed symbols, so it would be unnecessary for us to talk about, or for our artists to

---

[22]T. S. Eliot, "Ulysses, Order, and Myth," *The Modern Tradition: Backgrounds of Modern Literature,* eds. Richard Ellmann and Charles Feidelson, Jr. (New York: Oxford University Press, 1965), p. 681. Originally published in *The Dial,* 75 (1923): 480–83.

make self-conscious use of, myths if our culture had a mythic story in terms of which to live.

In "The Waste Land" Eliot makes use of an overwhelming number of references to mythology, theology, and other literary works. He says in "notes" that accompany the poem,

> Not only the title, but the plan and a good deal of the incidental symbolism of the poem were suggested by Miss Jessie L. Weston's book on the Grail legend: *From Ritual to Romance.* . . . To another work of anthropology I am indebted in general, one which has influenced our generation profoundly; I mean *The Golden Bough;* I have used especially the two volumes *Adonis, Attis, Osiris.* Anyone who is acquainted with these works will immediately recognize in the poem certain references to vegetation ceremonies.[23]

We also see, in the notes to the poem Eliot supplies, references to the Old and New Testaments, the legend of *Tristan und Isolde,* the archetypal figures represented in Tarot cards, Dante's *Divine Comedy,* Augustine's *Confessions,* and the Buddha's Fire Sermon — to mention only a few. Eliot is utilizing a large number of mythic sources (which may indicate a unitive world out of which they all come), which he interweaves with scenes from the twentieth century "waste land" that is really the subject of his poem.

As he indicates in the notes, the quest myth, especially in its paradigmatic form of the search for the Holy Grail, is the broadest mythic structure of the poem. Life-giving water is the symbol for what is lacking and what is sought. But the Waste Land lies largely in Frye's mythos of winter — the mythos of irony and the anti-hero, which is, it seems, most descriptive of our world. Thus the modern search for the Grail has to be true to our time. There can be no white knights or Sir Gawains rescuing the dry earth and the sterile lives of the people from their plight. And there can be no smashing victory, as we would expect to find in the mythos of romance. No, we live in the world of winter, of old age, that can only hope for hints of rebirth. The poem, then, presents archetypal images of great power and nobility alongside of and merging with accounts of our very mundane and superficial lives as they actually are in the waste land. One result of this juxtaposition is to illuminate, ironically, the barrenness of our own world. When the famed Sybil of Cumae, the guardian of sacred mysteries, becomes Madam Sosostris, a modern clairvoyant with her Tarot cards and horoscope readings; or when the archetypal image of the queen

[23]T. S. Eliot, *The Complete Poems and Plays* (New York: Harcourt, Brace and Co., 1958), p. 50.

revealed in all her splendor through the image of Cleopatra melts into a contemporary conversation in which the feminine figure now needs a new set of teeth and has injured her health through a self-induced abortion, the obvious incongruity between the two worlds hits us. We are made painfully aware of the absence of meaning as the images of our world are cut off from significant patterns.

However, if this were all that occurred in our experience of the poem, if there were only the negative accomplishment of showing us how far our world is from the greatness of mythic consciousness, then Eliot's hope that myth might make the modern world possible for art would not have been realized. The use of myth not only brings about a recognition of what has been lost; but, through mythopoesis, it also serves to begin the recovery. Stanley Romaine Hopper explains what happens in this way: Eliot is able to succeed in bringing the archetypal images present in the classical myths to life for us because he does not simply use allegory to connect the mythological and contemporary images. That is, we cannot equate this contemporary image with that classical myth. If we could, we would remain on an analytic level and just make the (negative) connections between the secular and mythic forms of consciousness. Eliot, instead, is able, through the mythological images, to reveal the mythic dimensions of our own, only apparently, secular lives. In doing this, as Hopper says,

> The Waste Land precipitated (as we now know many times over) "the unconscious awareness of an epoch." Which means that Eliot's poem contained beneath his skills that fortuitous thrust of autonomous psychical image formation that gave the poem almost immediately its singular place and influence in the poetic output of the first half of our century. Eliot's use of the Grail Legend . . . as governing and informing myth for his poem *did not function allegorically,* but opened up rather the way into the quest archetype of the Unconscious.[24]

The death images of the waste land and the rebirth themes from vegetation myths offer both the possibility of hope and the age-old experience of the hero who, through ordeal and darkness, achieves the possibility of new life.

James Joyce's *Ulysses* can be said to be working in much the same way. As the title indicates, Joyce uses Homer's *Odyssey* as the controlling mythic structure for his long novel. The sections, characters, events in *Ulysses* have their parallels in *The Odyssey*;

---

[24]Stanley Romaine Hopper, "Myth, Dream, and Imagination," *Myths, Dreams, and Religion,* ed. Joseph Campbell (New York: E.P. Dutton & Co., 1970), p. 125.

and, with much work and a helpful critic such as Stuart Gilbert, the reader can work out, almost allegorically, just what incident in Homer's work is the model for Joyce's. Since *Ulysses* takes place in modern day Dublin, with the hero now a very average character named Leopold Bloom, if there were only a comparison being made between ancient and modern or myth and secular, the novel could only depict, once again, the waste land of modern life. And indeed, as in Eliot's poem, this is *part* of what occurs in the novel as this critic reveals:

> *Ulysses* is one of the loneliest of books. The constant burden of Thomas Wolfe, "O lost, and by the wind grieved," is here set forth in comprehensive and objective terms. What in Wolfe seems the tragic cry of an individual soul is here a pervasive condition of modern civilization.[25]

But, as in Eliot's poem, something more is occurring as well. Through the overarching myth of *The Odyssey,* as well as through a seemingly endless number of other layers of our cultural past (all of Irish history, the Latin mass of the Church, all levels of language) that also structure the novel, Joyce succeeds in giving our ordinary lives a resonance of mythic meaning so that once more the quest is not fruitless but ends with hints of fecundity and new life.

Joyce collapses the many years and countless miles of the quest journey into eighteen hours of one day in Dublin. We follow the mundane experiences in that day of Stephen Daedalus and his "father" (by spiritual affinity rather than blood) Leopold Bloom. We see them in their travels through the city of Dublin, now apart, now coming together, as the search of the son for the father and the father for the son is pursued. Joyce gives us an overview of their lives, along with Dublin and Irish history, that allows us to see, as from a great height, what we could not see in the midst of our everyday lives: the patterns that make up our lives and connect them with structures of significance. Joyce's work is an epic for our time, as Homer's was for his. It is a very difficult work, and one is often tempted just to work at the level of unpacking the myriad references Joyce uses as he succeeds in being so totally inclusive of all Western civilization. However, the mythopoeic function of the novel occurs only at the level of experience as the novel gives expression to the ever present mythic structures of reality.

---

[25]Richard M. Kain, *Fabulous Voyager: James Joyce's Ulysses* (New York: The Viking Press, 1966), p. 72.

POETRY AND MYTH

Many of the explorers of modern culture, in a great variety of fields, agree with Yeats's poetic statement that "Things fall apart; the centre cannot hold," and with Eliot's waste land descriptions of modern culture. Certainly one sense in which this is true is, as revealed in the works of Joyce and Eliot, that our culture does not share a sacred story or myth that encompasses and gives meaning to our individual and collective lives. We live in a "waste land" just because we do not have living symbols that give expression to the depth dimension of experience and put us in touch with the source of a meaningful order in existence.

The response to life in the waste land is often lack of recognition or denial. We have so much it is often difficult to see that it is not things but greater patterns of significance in which we participate that give meaning to our lives. Sometimes the recognition does come—perhaps by having the veils of complacency stripped away; being confronted by the sense of loss, emptiness, anxiety; and knowing this is the waste land, the place of rock and no water. Although before this recognition we may try to flee from any hint that all is not well in our world, after the experience of broken images we know there is no escape. It will be in the waste land, if anywhere, that we finally encounter water. We must begin where we are and only wait to hear the word. As T. S. Eliot says in his poem "East Coker,"

> I said to my soul, be still, and wait without hope
> For hope would be hope for the wrong thing; wait without love
> For love would be love of the wrong thing; there is yet faith
> But the faith and the love and the hope are all in the waiting.
> Wait without thought, for you are not ready for thought:
> So the darkness shall be the light, and the stillness the dancing.[26]

But how can the darkness turn to light and the stillness to dancing? How can the word ever be spoken? We do not share a mythic language, and we acknowledge that one cannot be created by us. It must grow out of the resources of our culture and out of another dimension—which has been called the unconscious, the mythic, the sacred. Our problem is, however, that we are no longer in touch with this dimension. So how can it be restored? Martin Heidegger tells the story of our time in this way:

> It is the time of the gods that have fled *and* of the god that is coming. It is the time *of need,* because it lies under a double lack and a double Not: the

[26]T. S. Eliot, *Complete Poems and Plays*, pp. 126–27.

No-more of the gods that have fled and the Not-yet of the god that is coming.[27]

In such an in-between time Heidegger says we must listen to our poets. It is they who are able to "hail being" and to bring us into the "neighborhood of being." The poet, and poetry, thus take on central importance in our culture. They are our only guides back to the source of being. In some ways this idea parallels the Romantic view of the poet as priest and the Arnoldian belief in the power of art to save us. But it must be something different if is it to have the power to speak to our time, which is, of course, a distinctly different moment of history.

In order to understand this view of the poet we will begin by examining Cassirer's understanding of the origin of art. We must go back to his assumption that language and myth have a common root and that language also possesses, and has developed, a theoretical view of the world. In fact, it is this theoretical consciousness rather than the mythic consciousness that dominates our contemporary world. Along with the development of logic, however (whereby the potency of the word was lost as it became separated from the object), another development also occurred—that of art. Art was originally, like language, inseparable from myth. The narrative form itself, as well as dance, pictures, music—all were part of the "mythico-magic" world and were acknowledged only as they were used in its service. With the separation of art and language from myth, there was an inevitable loss of expression of immediate experience in language. But art is able to recover this experience on a higher, spiritual level wherein the word preserves its original creative power in an at once "sensuous and spiritual reincarnation." Cassirer says that lyric poetry

> most clearly mirrors this ideal development. For lyric poetry is not only rooted in mythic motives as its beginning, but keeps its connection with myth even in its highest and purest products. . . . The world of poetry stands apart from both [the mythic word-picture of gods and daemons and the logical truth of abstract determinations and relations], as a world of illusion and fantasy—but it is just in this mode of illusion that the realm of pure feeling can find utterance, and can therewith attain its full and concrete actualization.[28]

Jung also believes that the sources of art lie in the mythic origins of life—for him, the collective unconscious. With neither

---

[27]Martin Heidegger, "Hölderlin and the Essence of Poetry," trans. Douglas Scott, *Existence and Being*, 2nd ed. (London: Vision Press, 1956), p. 313.
[28]Cassirer, *Language and Myth*, p. 99.

Jung nor Cassirer does this mythic area involve a specific *content,* but whereas Cassirer is working from his idea of symbolic forms, Jung refers to "primordial experience" as the source of creativeness. This experience must necessarily take the form of mythological imagery since it cannot be logically conveyed, but this does not mean the poet takes on myths secondhand. Rather, he or she experiences them through the collective unconscious. Poetry is great, then, in so far as poets are able to open themselves to this mythical world and let it come to life through them. If the poet is successful, there will be a penetration

> to that matrix of life in which all men are embedded, which imparts a common rhythm to all human existence, and allows the individual to communicate his feeling and his striving to mankind as a whole.
>
> The secret of artistic creation and of the effectiveness of art is to be found in a return to the state of *participation mystique* — to that level of experience at which it is man who lives, and not the individual, and at which the weal or woe of the single human being does not count, but only human existence.[29]

Thus for Jung poetry takes on a mythical function, reuniting human beings with their origins and, in a timeless community, giving them new life.

We have seen the way Joyce and Eliot used mythology to make this realm Jung describes accessible to the modern world. Here we will look at yet another use of mythology, this time with our emphasis on the poet. In this case there is not only the conscious use of earlier mythologies but also the creation of a mythological world. In the poetry of William Butler Yeats and William Blake we sense that Jung's statement holds: these poets are not just using references to mythology but are writing from the experience of a total myth in which they are themselves involved. In each case the poet's encounter with the archetypes of the collective unconscious is expressed through a symbol system created by the poet. Even though both poets draw extensively on traditions from the past, one feels when reading the poetry that one has entered into their worlds. Being drawn into these worlds one is moved beyond the personal to the level where, as Jung says, all people live.

Both Yeats and Blake can be called "visionaries." Their sense of poetry is that it is the medium through which one can come to see the truth. It is not the intention of either of them to cloak a

[29]C. G. Jung, *Modern Man in Search of a Soul,* trans. W. S. Dell and Cary F. Baynes (New York: Harcourt, Brace and World, 1933), p. 172.

form of evangelism in poetry in order to get people to listen to them. Rather, it is the poet who can see; and it is poetry through which the vision can be expressed.

Although Blake and Yeats are very different poets and view the relationship of their poetry to mythology in different ways, they are alike in creating a cosmic vision that informs their poetry and makes it a revelation of archetypal truths that are universal and timeless. Each has a theory of history and a theory of the nature of human beings and divine Beings. There is a process by which history and nature are fulfilled and in which human nature is united with the divine. Thus, there is an image of wholeness that is understood to be not a personal preference of either man but an expression of the way things really are. But, you might say (and a critic like Northrop Frye would encourage you to say it), all poets, if examined in depth, would yield a similar wholeness of vision. On the individual level we could say that all poetry must present a consistent, total world view; it must grow out of a pattern of values if it is to have the wholeness that is a work of art. Or, as archetypal critics, we might say that the wholeness of vision must be there because all poets must work out of the archetypal possibilities that are the building blocks of all symbolism. Although within this view of literature we would affirm this as true, we select Yeats and Blake as paradigms because their accomplishment of this function of poetry is overt. There is a deliberate creation, or at least a deliberate use, of a symbol system to express just such a total view of human existence.

Blake, writing around the beginning of the nineteenth century, devotes a great part of his poetic creation to his longer poems, which he calls *The Prophecies*. The title is indicative of his view of these writings. He uses as his primary traditional source the Hebrew prophets of the Old Testament. They are his model, both as they present a vision of the world that the world does not want to see and as they experience the vision, the inner light—Ezekiel's "wheel" vision being a paradigm. Working from this source, Blake includes in his schema later occult and alchemical interpretations as well as the prophets' more practical, ethical precepts. He uses figures from any number of other symbol systems as well, interweaving them with his own, created mythological figures. He can do this because, as he believes, "all had originally one language, and one religion."[30] The poet,

---

[30]Northrop Frye, *Fearful Symmetry: A Study of William Blake* (Princeton: Princeton University Press, 1969), p. 420.

through the creation of a mythopoeic world, is therefore not creating new images or ideas, but revealing the truths that have always been. Thus Blake contains within his poetry the whole world.

William Butler Yeats wrote around the beginning of the twentieth century and, consequently, reflects more of the brokenness of our own time. He uses a wide range of classical mythological references in his poetry, but we will turn immediately to his prose work *A Vision* where his mythological system is elaborated. Yeats received the material for this work from his wife whom he married about half way through his poetic career. The vision came to Mrs. Yeats through automatic writing. Over a period of several years she was the medium through whom various personages (often adopting the names of household pets) communicated. The material was not foreign to images from Yeats's earlier poetry or from readings they had both done in the occult. The sources for the vision were sometimes felt by them to be other "spirits" and sometimes the wellsprings of Mrs. Yeats's unconscious. In any case what was given was an archetypal world that influenced the rest of Yeats's poetry substantially. He does not, however, simply try to reproduce the mythopoeic "system" in his poetry; it would no doubt have been stifling to his creativity if he had. But he sees the cosmic vision as a basic symbolic expression of the nature of reality that lies behind his poetic expression.

His image of the cosmos is spirals or gyres—a vortex image that is in constant motion, containing all opposites, continuing all life, and, at its opposite poles, offering moments of wholeness and stasis, which once again resolve into reincarnation and continuing movement. The vortices lie within a sphere, which is beyond movement, beyond the conflict of our experience of the world: a unified reality that ultimately provides the stability for our whirling world. The gyres give expression to an understanding of history as recurring and include all human history, the traditional four elements of the earth, the twenty-eight phases of the moon, the different occupations of human beings, the different personality types and forms of consciousness—in short, all natural and human phenomena find their place in the vision.

Through the openness of Mrs. Yeats to the unconscious (in this case seen as a true other, rather than part of herself), archetypal symbols reflecting the structures of being are brought to conscious realization and provide a basic symbol system for the mythopoeic world of W. B. Yeats.

When we move to the middle of the twentieth century we encounter another poet whose openness to the unconscious was a source for his poetry. Perhaps because he lived at a later time and in a different age from Blake and Yeats, Theodore Roethke's poetry is not built on the elaborate mythological structure we saw in the other two poets. Roethke reflects his time by offering us only glimpses of the archetypal world. The all-encompassing mythology of a Yeats may not be the way the archetypal vision can be revealed in our time. However, both Blake and Yeats are very important figures to Roethke. He was clearly attracted by the worlds they were able to create; and they become, with other great poets from the past, accesses to the Source for Roethke. They are the "ancestors," the dead, who "begin from their dark to sing in my sleep" ("Journey to the Interior"). They open the world of the unconscious that is the source of creativity. He records this experience of the importance of these "presences":

> Let me say boldly, now, that the extent to which the great dead can be evoked, or can come to us, can be eerie, and astonishing. . . .
> I was in that particular hell of the poet: a longish dry period. It was 1952, I was 44, and I thought I was done. . . .
> Suddenly, in the early evening, the poem "The Dance" started, and finished itself in a very short time—say thirty minutes, maybe the greater part of an hour, it was all done. I felt, I *knew*, I had hit it. I walked around, and I wept; and I knelt down—I always do after I've written what I know is a good piece. But at the same time I had, as God is my witness, the actual sense of a Presence—as if Yeats himself were *in* that room. The experience was in a way terrifying, for it lasted at least half an hour. That house, I repeat, was charged with a psychic presence: the very walls seemed to shimmer. I wept for joy. At last I was somebody again. He, they—the poets dead—were with me.[31]

It seems that for Roethke, as for many contemporary poets, to live close to such presences, to be open to the unconscious, is not only a positive source of creativity but also a great risk. Roethke had recurring bouts with mental illness of the manic-depressive type during which floods of exuberance or deadening lifelessness would overwhelm him. There seems to be no evidence that these periods were sources of creativity for his poetry; but it is possible that the same openness that allowed him to write out of the vast resources of the unconscious sometimes led to his being overwhelmed by this powerful reservoir of energy.

To be a poet in our time, then, seems a risky venture. Lacking a cohesive mythology shared by our culture, being unable to create one and still be true to our culture, the poet is called on to walk a narrow path and take the risk of encountering archetypal

---

[31]"On 'Identity,'" *On the Poet and His Craft: Selected Prose of Theodore Roethke,* ed. Ralph J. Mills, Jr. (Seattle: University of Washington Press, 1968), pp. 23–24.

reality without established forms of the tradition for protection. This is the situation of our poets as they attempt, in Heidegger's terms, to "hail Being." In Roethke's poetry this means taking the risk that no poetry will emerge. In some of his early poetry he commits himself to the exploration of the underground world of the unconscious, relying on association, nursery rhymes, almost gibberish, trusting, hoping that from this chthonic world an order will emerge, an occasion will come into being. And the joy that occurs in his poetry lies precisely in the event of the discovery that the risk is justified, that a structure of meaning supports and confirms the deepest sense of himself. Our response as readers is to share in this joy and marvel at this discovery and perhaps to entertain the possibility that such a structure of reality underlies our lives.

We see in the poem "In a Dark Time" a poetic description of the personal quest that runs the risk of failure—of the darkness and silence of nonbeing. The outcome of this "dark time" is, however, an experience of light and unity and the creation of a poem, a poem that touches the reality we may sense, though it is beyond our grasp.

In a dark time, the eye begins to see,
I meet my shadow in the deepening shade;
I hear my echo in the echoing wood—
A lord of nature weeping to a tree.
I live between the heron and the wren,
Beasts of the hill and serpents of the den.

What's madness but nobility of soul
At odds with circumstance? The day's on fire!
I know the purity of pure despair,
My shadow pinned against a sweating wall.
That place among the rocks—is it a cave,
Or winding path? The edge is what I have.

A steady storm of correspondences!
A night flowing with birds, a ragged moon,
And in broad day the midnight come again!
A man goes far to find out what he is—
Death of the self in a long, tearless night,
All natural shapes blazing unnatural light.

Dark, dark my light, and darker my desire.
My soul, like some heat-maddened summer fly,
Keeps buzzing at the sill. Which I is *I*?
A fallen man, I climb out of my fear.

The mind enters itself, and God the mind,
And one is One, free in the tearing wind.[32]

THE POET AS MEDIATOR

Martin Heidegger's description of the poet includes the risk we see in Roethke's poetry. Heidegger says ours is a time of need, the time of the absence of the gods, the world's night in which Being is silent. What this means is that we have no living mythology, no traditional symbols out of which we can live. Therefore, there must be risk and the possibility of failure as we seek to touch archetypal reality. Our usual, safe way of living in this dangerous time is to cut ourselves off from all possibilities of encountering Being, and in this way we also avoid the risk that encounter entails. We do this by treating everything as an object—important only as it can be used by us—that can be fully understood by quantitative means and is thus under our control. In our objectifying we include the Source of life itself. Being becomes a thing that can be manipulated and controlled by us as anything else. There will be no surprises, no mystery—and no real encounter. This may be safe; but, of course, to Heidegger it is to cut oneself off from the very Source of life. This is the forgetfulness of Being.

To move away from this objectifying view of the world we must begin with a reconception of Being itself. The language we use to describe the realm of the sacred makes it appear static—an object, a thing. But Being is not *any thing*. It is *no-thing*. Yet it enables all things to be. To come into the presence of the sacred is to encounter the potentiality of all that is through *attending to* what is "at hand." This is the opposite of *using* what is "to hand," which is the objectifying mode. The true way of being in the world is to let things be for us as they are. When we do and when we attend very closely to things as they are, we may come into the presence of Being.

But how are we to do this? In this time when Being is concealed, when such a risk is demanded to step into the nothingness, we must turn to our poets—our artists—as guides. Heidegger says in the essay "What Are Poets For?": "To be a poet in a destitute time means: to attend, singing, to the trace of the fugitive gods."[33] The poet is willing to venture into the region of

---

[32] *The Collected Poems of Theodore Roethke* (Garden City, N.Y.: Doubleday & Co., 1966), p. 239.
[33] Martin Heidegger, "What Are Poets For?" *Poetry, Language, Thought,* trans. Albert Hofstadter (New York: Harper & Row, 1975), p. 94.

the unknown, the mystery that grounds all of existence even though it remains concealed. The poet stands before the mystery, stands in the open, with an attitude of releasement toward things or *Gelassenheit* (letting be). Not asserting his will on the world but attending closely to what is given, he comes into the presence of Being—Being that is not a thing but the possibility of all beings being. It is not in silence that the poet comes, but through language he "hails the integrity of the globe of Being."[34] Through the poetry that results when the poet attends to the Being that is given, the two realms of the sacred and the secular are brought together. His singing over the land hallows. It hails Being and it brings those who hear into the neighborhood of Being.

The poet Rainer Maria Rilke says in *Sonnets to Orpheus* (1st pt., 3), "Gesang ist Dasein;" "song is existence." The poet Hölderlin says,

dichterish wohnet
Der Mensch auf dieser Erde.

("In lieblichner Bläue . . .")

poetically
Man dwells upon the earth.

These are occasions of the hailing of Being, and they are also descriptions of how we hail Being. In them, *aletheia,* the unveiling or disclosing that is the poet's vocation, occurs. We dwell on the earth through song, through poetry, because poetry is the most vital expression in our time of meditative thinking. This is the thinking, as opposed to calculative thinking, that stands with awe before the things of the world and is astonished by the fact that there is something rather than nothing. This is the kind of thinking that does not try to manipulate and fit things into categories so they can be controlled by human reason. It simply allows things to be.[35] Thinking in this sense is thanking, for to be aware of the givenness of things is to experience gratitude for the gift. In German, "Denken ist Danken": "Thinking is thanking."

The *aletheia* or unveiling that occurs in this act of thanksgiving is truth, which is a trait of Being. Truth is not a static thing that can be an object of knowledge but is rather an occurrence. Since Being itself always remains transcendent, the disclosure that is the truth must always come by way of the things of this world. Yet it

---

[34]Ibid., p. 141.
[35]Cf. Martin Heidegger, *Discourse on Thinking: A Translation of "Gelassenheit,"* trans. John M. Anderson and E. Hans Freund (New York: Harper & Row, 1966), *passim.*

must come through the things of the world metaphorically rather than literally. Poetry, which deals with the concrete particularity of the world through metaphor and symbol, is the perfect medium for the unveiling that is truth. However, even in the unconcealing, there remains a concealedness, just as the word *aletheia* contains within it *lethe* or concealedness.[36] The hidden remains hidden, even as it is brought to light. Being is the transcendent source by which all things are lighted up. But the source remains transcendent and remains concealed.

> Though Being is always given in, with, and through its appearances, it is not itself simply appearance, since it is that which enables things, as it were, to be gathered together and to stand before us: so it must in some sense be concealed.[37]

So poetically we dwell on the earth. We dwell in the house of language, we hail Being through words, through song. To *dwell* is to live fully in the presence of beings and thus of Being. The poet as the Watchman or Shepherd of Being teaches us to pay heed to beings in all their uniqueness and particularity. In so doing he brings us into the presence of Being.

> The poet calls all the brightness of the sights of the sky and every sound of its courses and breezes into the singing word and there makes them shine and ring. Yet the poet, if he is a poet, does not describe the mere appearance of sky and earth. The poet calls, in the sights of the sky, that which in its very self-disclosure causes the appearance of that which conceals itself, and indeed *as* that which conceals itself. In the familiar appearances, the poet calls the alien as that to which the invisible imparts itself in order to remain what it is—unknown.[38]

Although Heidegger is a philosopher rather than a poet, his use of language contains many of the qualities we attribute to poetry. In order for his writing to reflect his thinking he must proceed by questions more than answers, by hints that leave a sense of mystery rather than by exposition that explains without remainder. His work must reflect the *process* of thinking more than a static *what* that is thought. And finally he uses a great deal of poetry— most often Rilke and Hölderlin—to present for experience what cannot be baldly stated. Because poetry can hail Being, it is the

---

[36]Cf. Werner Marx, "Poetic Dwelling and the Role of the Poet," *On Heidegger and Language,* ed. and trans. Joseph J. Kockelmans (Evanston: Northwestern University Press, 1972), pp. 238–39.

[37]Nathan A. Scott, Jr., *The Wild Prayer of Longing: Poetry and the Sacred* (New Haven: Yale University Press, 1971), p. 69.

[38]Heidegger, "'. . . Poetically Man Dwells . . .,'" *Poetry, Language, Thought,* p. 225.

task of the true thinker to be the mediator, the poet—who discloses, who unconceals, who "names the Holy"—that in this time of dearth, we may be brought into the Presence.

Radical Immanence and Myth in Contemporary Poetry

Stanley Hopper describes our time as the time of the crisis of the mythological imagination. He quotes from Friedrich Schelling's *Philosophie der Mythologie*:

> The crisis through which the world and the history of the gods develop is not outside the poets; it takes place in the poets themselves, it *makes* their poems . . . it is the crisis of the mythological consciousness which in entering into them makes the history of the gods.[39]

Schelling is discussing the developments in Greece that gave rise to both their first poets and a fully developed history of the gods. Our "crisis of the mythological consciousness," although comparable, is in some ways quite different:

> Certainly the crisis is not outside our poets and artists, but is decisively *in* them and makes their poems and artworks. But their works are strange: are seemingly antiheroic and antimythical—they celebrate not a differentiation of the gods so much as their repudiation, and the "liberation" that we feel comes not from more precise delineation of the godly pantheon but from refusing it obeisance in the forms that we have known heretofore. . . . The liberation that we feel rejoices in our release from ways of knowing and seeing that had become too oppressive:
>
>> "It was when I said,
>> 'There is no such thing as the truth,'
>> That the grapes seemed fatter.
>> The fox ran out of his hole."[40]

The radical immanence of the mythological vision of our time must necessarily appear to be anti-mythological. As in the quotation from Wallace Stevens above, it is the rejection of absolutes, of that which is transcendent of the reality we know, that makes that reality and our lives take on new meaning. However, as in Heidegger's thought, it is through seeing things as they are and letting things be as they are that a new movement from reality to Reality is possible. Thus, there is not a rejection of the mythological imagination in our time but a new approach to it.

The way of Wallace Stevens is one of these new approaches. Stevens writes out of the situation Heidegger describes. The old

---

[39]Stanley Romaine Hopper, "Myth, Dream, and Imagination," p. 111.
[40]Ibid., p. 112. The poetry is from Wallace Stevens's "On the Road Home."

forms that gave shape to our world have broken; we are left in a difficult in-between time with immanent reality—with our world. It is for our poets to create "supreme fictions" by which we may live: to order our reality with aesthetic forms. These aesthetic forms, however, seem to open out on something beyond them—the mythological order we have been considering in this chapter.

Stevens's poem "Sunday Morning" presents our moment of loss as well as hints of recovery. It reveals a woman lounging at home on a Sunday morning, thinking and dreaming about the old forms of Christianity that are still a part of her, even though they are now seen negatively. She imagines other possibilities that might be more life-giving: the ancient gods, who were more playful and more "human" or the natural world, especially the sun, which is a paradigm or archetype of the source of life that touches all of life. The poem begins:

I

Complacencies of the peignoir, and late
Coffee and oranges in a sunny chair,
And the green freedom of a cockatoo
Upon a rug mingle to dissipate
The holy hush of ancient sacrifice.
She dreams a little, and she feels the dark
Encroachment of that old catastrophe,
As a calm darkens among water-lights.
The pungent oranges and bright, green wings
Seem things in some procession of the dead,
Winding across wide water, without sound.
The day is like wide water, without sound,
Stilled for the passing of her dreaming feet
Over the seas, to silent Palestine,
Dominion of the blood and sepulchre.

II

Why should she give her bounty to the dead?
What is divinity if it can come
Only in silent shadows and in dreams?
Shall she not find in comforts of the sun,
In pungent fruit and bright, green wings, or else
In any balm or beauty of the earth,
Things to be cherished like the thought of heaven?
Divinity must live within herself:
Passions of rain, or moods in falling snow;
Grievings in loneliness, or unsubdued
Elations when the forest blooms; gusty
Emotions on wet roads on autumn nights;
All pleasures and all pains, remembering
The bough of summer and the winter branch.
These are the measures destined for her soul.

And yet her vision is not untroubled. She is still wed to the old and at the same time uncertain about this new dream.

> She says, "But in contentment I still feel
> The need of some imperishable bliss."

And the following lines in the poem say, "Death is the mother of beauty." We are torn between our affirmation of the vital, living process of our world and our longing for that which does not change.

Thus, it is clear in Stevens's poem that the old forms, the church steeples, no longer suffice. But the new way is also a way of darkness, uncertainty, and risk as we see in the final stanza of the poem:

> VIII
> She hears, upon that water without sound,
> A voice that cries, "The tomb in Palestine
> Is not the porch of spirits lingering.
> It is the grave of Jesus, where he lay."
> We live in an old chaos of the sun,
> Or old dependency of day and night,
> Or island solitude, unsponsored, free,
> Of that wide water, inescapable.
> Deer walk upon our mountains, and the quail
> Whistle about us their spontaneous cries;
> Sweet berries ripen in the wilderness;
> And, in the isolation of the sky,
> At evening, casual flocks of pigeons make
> Ambiguous undulations as they sink,
> Downward to darkness, on extended wings.[41]

In another poem, "Esthetique du Mal," we see again the ambiguity and another characteristic of much of Stevens's poetry, irony. But we also see again the affirmation of the world and the sense that lying behind it, shining through it, are things as they are.

> The greatest poverty is not to live
> In a physical world. . . .
> The green corn gleams and the metaphysicals
> Lie sprawling in majors of the August heat,
> The rotund emotions, paradise unknown.
>
> This is the thesis scrivened in delight,
> The reverberating psalm, the right chorale.

---

[41]Wallace Stevens, *The Palm at the End of the Mind: Selected Poems and a Play,* ed. Holly Stevens (New York: Random House, Vintage Books Edition, 1972), pp. 5–8. The following quotations are taken from this edition.

One might have thought of sight, but who could think
Of what it sees, for all the ill it sees?
Speech found the ear, for all the evil sound,
But the dark italics it could not propound.
And out of what one sees and hears and out
Of what one feels, who could have thought to make
So many selves, so many sensuous worlds,
As if the air, the mid-day air, was swarming
With the metaphysical changes that occur,
Merely in living as and where we live. (Pp. 262–63)

Finally, in Stevens's poetry we see the poet, struggling to write the poem, to be the poem, to hear the poem that is the world. Usually he must laugh a little at himself, and us at him, for he is fairly bumbling in his efforts and realizes, if he really is a poet, that the goal always exceeds his reach. This is inevitable in a reality that is characterized by change. So the poet is a comedian, a voyager, a creator of supreme fictions, who can laugh at himself and at his world, who is always a little ironic, who does not deny the darkness but can bear it all because he knows the central poem is being written and writing him:

That's it. The lover writes, the believer hears,
The poet mumbles and the painter sees,
Each one, his fated eccentricity,
As a part, but part, but tenacious particle,
Of the skeleton of the ether, the total
Of letters, prophecies, perceptions, clods
Of color, the giant of nothingness, each one
And the giant ever changing, living in change.
("A Primitive Like an Orb," p. 320)

With the understanding that "poetry" refers to all the literary arts, we can see another response to this in-between time in the novels of John Barth. The old mythological forms abound in *The Sot-Weed Factor* and *Giles Goat-Boy,* but in such a different way that they and our attitude toward them are totally transformed. *The Sot-Weed Factor* gives us our history—through the paradigm of American history; *Giles Goat-Boy* gives us our future. In both cases myths are used extensively but are reinterpreted so we might look at them from a new perspective of irony—and may in this way improve our vision. The transcendent "gods" are brought firmly down to earth and their fallibility clearly shown. There is a great deal of darkness in Barth's novels, but there is also a great deal of laughter. The main characters—they cannot be called heroes—must have their dreams disrupted and face disillusionment, for "nothing is as it seems." And the hope at the end for a

new vision—new forms that can shape reality, new access to a
meaningful order—if it comes at all, only shimmers behind the
possibility of resignation to meaninglessness.

Barth uses our mythologies to tear us away from them. We
must come to see that they no longer have the power to give our
lives meaning, and we must stop pretending that they do. He
makes us laugh, however, even as we, with the characters, feel the
pain. In Northrop Frye's structure we may see (with both Stevens
and Barth) a movement through the mythos of winter toward that
of spring—from biting irony to gentler satire that moves gradually
into comedy. The darkness of winter is surely still there but so, it
seems, is the affirmation to live with that darkness, and, perhaps,
to find something to affirm there.

David Miller is a final figure we will look at in this regard.
Miller is not a poet, but a thinker who must be like a poet in
Heidegger's terms. Miller takes the in-between time seriously in
both its darkness and its immanence. He follows the Jungian
model of turning inward to the unconscious to discover the
sources of Being; and he uses, among other things, the drama of
classical Greece to help us discover our own story in the ancient
myths. For example, using Aristophanes' play *The Frogs* Miller
describes how our journey, like that of Dionysos, must be into the
darkness of Hades. It is in the shadow world, our own interior
darkness, that we may begin to see. We too must cross the
"depthless river" when the bottom drops out and we have no
refuge. And we must do it ourselves—with the help of poetry. The
idea, in Miller's interpretation, is not to overcome the darkness
but to learn to live in it. It is shadow that is the "very stuff of
soul." Shadow is the sub-stance that undergirds and gives body to
life. And what we do when we learn to see in the dark is poetry.
When one sees the depths, one can speak of them only metaphorically. To bring them to the light of day of literal discourse is to
have them vanish. Poetizing is, then, *skiopoiēsis*—making dark,
deepening.[42]

Miller seems to affirm the time of darkness, the time of the
abyss. It is only in the darkness that the word can be spoken. We
might see this as a movement back through the mythos of winter
into tragedy, which is the mythos of autumn, except that *The Frogs*
is a comedy. Dionysos who makes the journey to Hades is quite a
laughable character. He, a god, pretends to be a mortal. We who
make the interior journey may be just as laughable because as

---

[42]David L. Miller, "Hades and Dionysos: The Poetry of Soul," *Journal of the
American Academy of Religion* 46, no. 3 (September 1978): 331–35.

mortals we often make the pretense of being gods. There is also irony present in the fact that the play is about the inability to write plays any longer and it is a comedy using jokes that are no longer funny. The irony is further present in the language Miller has to use to interpret the play for our lives. We must learn to see in the dark, the in-visible reveals what is within, and what is seen and revealed is beyond the reach of language. So the poet and the thinker must speak in metaphor that does not overcome the ambiguity of the darkness that lets us see. Thus, we remain in the mythos of irony and satire, the mythos of winter, with traces of the mythos of tragedy and hints of the mythos of comedy.

THE IN-BETWEEN TIME

As we come to the end of this study of the relationship between literature and religion, we are using the language of one particular approach; but we find ourselves in a place that is perhaps characteristic of all the approaches because it is, for the most part, where we are at this particular moment in history. Throughout the study we have concentrated on modern Western literature in the hope of better understanding the manifestations of religion in our culture. Because our culture depends so greatly on the Hebrew and Christian traditions, we have continued to come back to resources from these traditions—as have our artists. If we had taken for our focus religious dimensions of Japanese culture, for example, our resources would obviously have come from the literary and religious traditions of that culture.

However, although the great traditions of our culture have been important, we have seldom found them expressed in unambiguous ways. As we have looked at the relationships between religion and literature through four angles of vision—religious themes, possibility, dialogue, and mythopoesis—we have discovered recurring characteristics and concerns that show us that the religious dimensions of our culture often remain only partially unconcealed. It has been necessary each step of the way to acknowledge the overlapping of these four angles of vision: they are not four distinct approaches that lead to four different conclusions, but rather four ways of looking at our culture that often require each other and tend to point to the same discoveries about the religious dimensions of our time.

The metaphor of the in-between time may be the best way to characterize what we have discovered about our culture. Frye's description of the mythos of winter, the time of irony (sometimes tending back toward tragedy) and of satire (sometimes tending forward toward comedy), also seems appropriate to our moment. In such a time it is not the surety of absolutes but the ambiguity of hints of the sacred, of possibilities of the More, that dominate our culture. It is a time that looks to the immanent, to what is, for glimpses of what might be. Because of this, ours is not a time for dogmatic assertions but rather a time for entertaining possibilities, for telling stories, which, through the multivalence of language, may point to, but cannot contain, the sacred that grounds our lives. In such a time it is appropriate that we have constantly returned to the role of language in our discussions. It is clear that it is the language of symbol and metaphor, which is the language of myth and story, that helps us to understand our relationship to the sacred. The language of symbols does not suggest that our access to the sacred is cut off but rather that there remains a concealedness and thus an element of irony in all our expressions of the religious quest. Stanley Hopper quotes Santayana:

> "Every concept is framed in its own irony." The same, unfortunately, is true of symbolic forms. Are all of these thoughtful forms caught in a struggle with the essentially metaphorical character of language, in which what is said both reveals and conceals its meaning?[43]

It is appropriate that Hopper should leave us with a question, for that, more than ambiguous answers, is characteristic of our time. What we can see so clearly in this in-between time is that there is always a residual irony in our aesthetic forms. There is always the *more* our poets may hint at and point to through their creations using religious themes, possibility, dialogue, and mythopoesis. But the Being that is hailed through a radical immanence is only partially unconcealed.

Paul Ricoeur describes this characteristic of language by pointing to the semantic structure of metaphorical language. A metaphor calls one thing something else. It creates a tension between two incongruous realities, helping us by this tension to see something new. But in the very act of saying "this is that," one indirectly says "This is *not* that."[44] The "is" and "is not" of metaphor is indeed a metaphor for the in-between time we discover in literature to be expressive of the religious dimensions of our culture.

It seems appropriate to end this discussion of the relationships between religion and literature with a story, told in Stefan George's poem "Das Wort" and retold and commented on by

---

[43]Hopper, "Myth, Dream, and Imagination," pp. 127–28.
[44]Paul Ricoeur, *Interpretation Theory: Discourse and the Surplus of Meaning* (Fort Worth: Texas Christian University Press, 1976), p. 69.

another poet and thinker, Stanley Hopper. George's poem tells of the poet who

> took his dreams to the gray Norn who sat by a deep well. From the well the Norn would draw out names for the poet's dreams. With these names the poet wrote his easy poems. But one day the poet brought a jewel in his hand. The goddess of fate sought long after the name for the jewel. At last she said to the poet: "For such there sleep nothing (no thing, no name) in the deep ground." Sadly the poet returned from his journey. "I learned," he said sadly, "No thing is where the Word is broken."

Like the poet, we manipulate words, control our meaning, contrive our patterns. But when we ask for the essence of speech (the jewel), the deep well does not comply: there is no name for it, it cannot be converted to a thing, it is not subject to my manipulation. The Word is given, it is not at our disposal. My words today are broken symbols. We know, after our fashion, that no thing is where the Word is broken. We must learn again, this time from the depth, to hear the Word that resounds through our words.[45]

---

[45]Hopper, "Myth, Dream, and Imagination," p. 137.

INDEX